YIELD

THE ART OF DRAWING CLOSER

"A 30 day devotional of inspiration, decree's, and prayers focusing on the power of yielding and opening oneself to the Holy Spirit."

Carnail Stokes Jr.

Published By: Stokes International Inc. © 2018

Copyright © 2018 by Carnail Stokes Jr.

All rights reserved. This book or any portion thereof may not be reproduced or used in any manner whatsoever without the express written permission of the publisher except for the use of brief quotations in a book review or scholarly journal.

First Printing: 2018

ISBN: 978-1984930811

Stokes International Inc.
PO BOX 28988
St. Paul, MN 55128-6127

www.stokesinternational.org

Ordering Information:

Special discounts are available on quantity purchases by corporations, associations, educators, and others. For details, contact the Publisher at the above listed address.

U.S. trade bookstores and wholesalers: Please contact Carnail Stokes Jr. for Stokes International Publishing Tel: (612) 460-1502 or email connect2stokes@gmail.com

TABLE OF CONTENTS

INTRODUCTION	8
Practical Application to Yield	14
The Structure of Yield	16
YIELD DEVOTIONAL	18
Day One- Yield to your Counsel	19
Day Two- Yield to your Leadership	29
Day Three- Yield to your direction	37
Day Four- Yield to your Strength	44
Day Five- Yield to your Lordship	51
Day Six- Yield to your Lordship pt 2	59
Day Seven- Yield to your Protection	67
Day Eight- Yield to your Truth and Word	75
Day Nine- Yield to your forgivemenss	83
Day Ten- Yield to your Joy	91
Day Eleven- Yield to your Timing	97
Day Twelve- Yield to your Holiness	103
Day Thirteen- Yield to your Fathering	110
Day Fourteen- Yield to your Spirit	116
Day Fifteen- Yield to your Grace	123
Day Sixteen- Yield to your Provision	130
Day Seventeen- Yield to your Breakthrough	136
Day Eighteen- Yield to your Sending	144
Day Nineteen- Yield to your Love	151
Day Twenty- Yield to your Glory	159
Day Twenty-One- Yield to your Covenant (the Blood)	165
Day Twenty-Two- Yield to your Humility	172
Day Twenty-Three- Yield to your Patience	179
Day Twenty-Four- Yield to your Revenge	185
Day Twenty-Five- Yield to your Usage	191
Day Twenty-Six- Yield to your Deliverance	197
Day Twenty-Seven- Yield to your Infilling	204
Day Twenty-Eight- Yield to your Baptism	211
Day Twenty-Nine- Yield to your Burden	218
Day Thirty- Yield to your Praise	224
BIBLIOGRAPHY	231

YIELD

THE POWER OF YIEDLING

Introduction:
The Power of Yielding

This is something I've never felt before. I lost all control. Something broke in me as if I was walking on a frozen lake and I had fell through (the ice). But I wasn't trying to swim to the surface. Deeper I went waiting for more, expecting more. It's beyond emotion, yet there is an armament of them inside of me. I'm hungry yet I am full. Thirsty but satisfied. This intoxicating presence overwhelmed me. He was no longer far away and I was no longer trying to run after Him. He was there with me and I with Him. A fountain of years, secrets, hurts, pains, adversities, questions, wondering thoughts were now, in that moment, all silenced by His presence.

I found myself holding on to it. Not wanting to let go of it. Deeper I went. There was no time, there was no me. The only thing that existed was He. I found everything in my being longing for Him. The depths of my soul reached for Him. Tears transformed into crying, crying progressed into weeping, and weeping erupted into groans. There was no subsiding, and I didn't want it to subside. I finally had Him because He had me. Without me asking, He released Himself to me because I gave myself to Him. In this moment, I no longer resisted Him I yielded to Him.

Behold my eyes were opened. I'm seeing what I have never seen. Hearing what I have never heard. This wasn't just about Him taking my sin or my shame. He was taking me completely. Laying me to rest and awaking me in Him. I was killed off that day that Christ might live in me. There was no asking He demanded this of me. DEAD to myself: alive in Him. I couldn't feel me anymore. There was no locating me. What is this idea called me or I? It doesn't exist in this place.

The only thing that exists is He. DEAD! That's what this was. My yielding brought me to my death. I had met my expiration. DEAD! And I knew I couldn't rise again. I, Carnail, die that death everyday in everything. It is a death I have willingly died. Knowing that to die is to meet resurrection.

That was just the beginning of the encounter I had that day in my room. The whole house was sleep while I was up seeking. Not fully understanding what seeking was, but knowing it was my portion and I had to do it. Oh how many of us profess Christ but yet you haven't yielded to the God you profess. You might be reading this thinking," What real importance does this have?" Well, to be honest yielding is everything. We say that we represent Christ but the only thing that we see is you. Your nature your expression. The only time that we have the slightest idea that you are His is when you open your mouth and share your passed down, second hand, back pocket with lent on it information that you heard from a preacher you didn't even understand. And even once shared you present Him- Yah as if he is a character in a novel, a statue that was built not someone you wake up with everyday. A lot of us that have professed and confess Christ have not received Christ.

This is not a question of sincerity it's a matter of how much of your life did you really give to Christ? If you truly gave Him all, then why are you still the captain, the decision maker, the leader, the controller? You still have the dominant role in your life, not knowing that in your weakness His strength is made perfect. There is no negotiating or debating, He wants and requires all of you.

John 15:4 *"Abide in me, and I in you. As the branch cannot bare fruit of itself, except it abide in the vine; no more can ye, except ye abide in me."* KJVS Here, God made us a promise that if we abide in Him that He would abide in us. But the Father then goes to show us the benefit of abiding in Him, fruit. There is a key here! Your ability to harvest Godly results waits on your direct connection to the Father; just, as a branch would be connected to the vine. We came to Him just to join His covenant with our idols, thinking that if we compartmentalize ourselves we can still have the actions, thoughts, and comforts of our past while still pursuing a Spirit led life. IT DOSEN'T WORK! One desire is going to have to die to the other.

There is a dangerous mentality in us fracturing our connection to the vine. This mentality prolongs growth, strangles maturity, forbids trust, and cripples obedience. In order to understand this subtle but fatal mentality you must understand this first. Our culture and time has been defined and shaped by words. With every generation, there are certain phrases that can be said that connect with a certain period of time. If I said, " shake a tale feather," you are going to think early 70's. Words have meaning and define mentality. When most of us gave our lives to Christ, we most likely heard a phrase such as, " Surrender your life to Christ." Well, if you were a sinner, that is a proper mentality however; it's not the way a Son or Daughter builds their relationship with the Father.

Though yield and surrender may seem like the same word, they are significantly different. Surrender in its simplest terms is to: *end resistance to an opponent or enemy and concede to their authority or power.* To yield means to: *willingly give to a superior authority or power.* Another meaning of yield is to: *produce or bear.* Looking at these definitions, we find it clear that to surrender means there is resistance but when you yield, willingness is your cause. YES! When we were sinners, we met a power greater than us, so we surrender. But now that you are His, you must learn to willingly give yourself.

Most of our walks with God whether just beginning or our tenure is long, have experienced constant surrender. Why? Because, there is a constant resistance in the flesh that doesn't want to willingly give up the things we use to comfort ourselves from our false realities. The resistance acts as a force field, allowing the idols of your life to be under arm and guard preserving their time of rule. Most saints of the Most

High are still constrain in past failures, disappointments, and regrets not because Christ is not available, but it is we ourselves who is not available. Preaching unavailable, singing unavailable, prophesying unavailable. We still think that we can fool God with our gifts not understanding that those things are without repentance. You can use them and still NOT BE AVAILABLE. What good is your gift or calling without you present.

I'm not saying that choosing to yield to Holy Spirit will always be easy, however it is necessary. Mark 8:36 affirm this by saying what will it profit you to gain the world and loose your soul. Yes, you will loose it because you where never present your gift was. We saw your talent but where are you hiding? Is it in addiction, some ones spouse, a fear, anger, divorce? Where are you hiding? Or in other words, what part of you is still resisting God from not just being the Lord of your outer man but your inner man. He doesn't want to just be Lord of your confession, He's ready to be Lord of your life.

At Jesus' most fierce moment, facing the world's powers and authorities, look at what Jesus says when His life is on the line, " *No man taketh it from me, but I lay it down of myself. I have the power to lay it down, and I have power to take it again. This commandment have I received of my Father.*"- John 10:18 KJV'S Our example Jesus, teaches us something so powerful. That even when your life is on the line, when it comes to the will of the Father, willingly give yourself. No man took Jesus life, HE GAVE IT! That same measure is asked of you. Give yourself willingly that Christ might be glorified in you. Give yourself willingly that all things can be made well in Gods timing.

Your resistance has prolonged your growth. Resistance applied in the wrong area can cleft your divine timing and yield enclosing cycles that soon become strong holds. Resistance can summons fear to join its crusade of keeping a barrier between you and the Father. This resistance doesn't necessarily have to be eliminated in your life just corrected. *"Submit yourselves therefore to God. Resist the devil, and he will flee from you."-James 4:7 KJVS* That same resistance that you once had towards God (whether knowingly or unknowingly) now becomes a barricade between you and the enemy. That same power called resistance that was once an enemy has now become a weapon. Notice that James tells us to submit to God. Submitting to God is an act that is done willingly.

In the verses leading up to this compelling statement, you will find that James is voicing the war that is going on inside of the believer. He then states that God resists the proud. That word resists means to range in battle against, to oppose. Oh, how many of us continued in the proud way; to make ourselves higher than those around us; even the direction of God. Proud in thinking that we know the way that we should take. We have become prideful in convincing ourselves that we have our best interest in mind. No! This is not an option this is a command. SUBMIT YOURSELVES THEREFORE UNTO GOD! Submit yourself that your thoughts might be established. Submit yourself that your days might be preserved. Submit yourself that the plan of God might be fulfilled in your life. There is joy in submitting. Why wage a war with the one who is stronger than all. The days of opposing Him must end.

"Humble yourself in the sight of the Lord, and he shall life you up."-
KJS James 4:10
"Humble yourselves [feeling very insignificant] in the presence of the Lord, and He will exalt you [He will left you up and make your lives significant]. -AMP- James 4:10

Humble. Meaning to make you low. Humbling yourself is yet another word where you give yourself willing. Casting yourself upon the mercy of the one you are before. We have come upon a day, that was, and now is, where man must bow their knee to He that is the King of all. We must not forget that God will not share His glory with another. He demands that we willingly give ourselves that His glory may be revealing in your uprising.

God is not requiring us to know the way, but He does want us to know Him. The more that we draw near to Him the more He will draw near to us, and in Him is the way. Remember, Jesus declared, *"... I am the way, the truth, and the life: no man cometh into the Father, but by me."* When you yield, you no longer have the responsibility for needing to know the way. The demand that life places on you daily is now exchanged at the altar of yielding. He, Christ takes that care and becomes your way and your only way. He doesn't just long to do this until you reach a place of knowing. He wants you to have constant reliance on His spirit, every day, every moment of that day, in constant awareness of Him. Let's yield together.

Practical Application to Yield

When wanting to materialize a greater place of yielding you must first acknowledge the places of resistances. This begins the divorce between you and what you desire. Confront yourself with the truth; by initially acknowledging the areas in your life that you have not yielded to the Father. Secondly, you must confess with your mouth that these areas still oppose the will of God in your life. By confessing, you bring those areas into the light of Gods word. You can do this by speaking to someone that you are accountable to or in prayer.

Now, it is my suggestion that you do both. There is no greater way to humble you then by making yourself vulnerable to another. Also prayer gives you platform to bare all before the Father, and that is the purpose of yielding; to bare all of yourself before Him knowing that He already knows all. Thirdly, conclude these areas by renouncing them and submit them to the nature of God. This is where the power of your confession is most important. By making declarations you are not just confessing the place of yielding, but you are instituting what shall be. Declaration is a formal announcement, a proclamation, and an edict. Daily announcing the places that you are yielding to fortifies the divorce of the former thing and prophecies to what is to be. Lastly, cultivate those areas by praying in the spirit. *"But ye, beloved, building up yourselves on your most holy faith, praying in the Holy Ghost."-KJVS Jude 1:20* By praying in the Holy Ghost you allow the Spirit to make intercession for you. The building of yourself by prayer is two fold; you yield and Christ builds you and fills you at the same time.

"Yea doubtless, and I count all things but loss for the excellency of the knowledge of Jesus Christ my Lord: for whom I have suffered the loss of all things, and do count them but dung, that I may win Christ." KJV S Phi. 3:8

This is one of the most powerful verses for anyone that seeks to demonstrate He, The Holy Ghost. Paul takes us into his personal experience on how he views the things of his life compared to Christ. Everything that predates Christ is counted as a loss. Not to say that it was a loss, but it more so means to purge himself of all - to lose it that he might have Christ. I mean can you see the pain yet the power in this statement. Paul is saying that my former reality of all that I am and all that I have obtained, everything that I know, everything that I hope to be, I lost it that I might seize a greater reality; and that is Christ.

Christianity on a large scale has been determined by moral good and not how much Christ is within. We are identified as Christian when we accept this faith, Christ-en or in. How much is Christ within? Again, we are to:

1. **Confront**- acknowledging the areas in your life that need to be yielded to God.
2. **Confess**- by speaking to an accountability partner or spiritual authority; this also can be done by confessing in a place of prayer.
3. **Conclude**- renounces the areas that you have not yielded to God and submit them to the nature of God.
4. **Cultivate**- Building your faith and awareness by declarations and prayer

THE STRUCTURE OF YIELD

The focus *Yield* is to bring the art of yield to life, by not only unveiling this truth but also giving you the foundational tools to effectively yield. As you continue to read, you will find daily inspirational readings that will be accompanied with scriptures that coincide with that day's topic. Following the scriptures you will have declarations and to conclude, a player that you can read to learn and open the dialogue of yielding prayers. The scriptures will be what we use to build our yielding prayer. I teach all over the country that your prayer is not legal unless it is founded upon the word of God. So, we will put this into practice. At first it might feel different, however as you continue it is a habit that can be adopted into your everyday prayer life.

Now even though these days are numbered they are not calendar days. Meaning that if you want to stay on day one for more than one day you can! This will give you the opportunity to invoke change and break certain strongholds within yourself. And find time to go read some of those foundational scriptures that are presented in that day. There will be areas presented at the conclusion of the written material to reflect. You can write certain scriptures, notes, difficulties with that yielding area, or your own personal declarations. It's a place for you to reflect.

Lastly, we want to insure that daily we have set the stage for you to offer yourself to the Father. Thus, the first ten days I have structured for you. After that I will start the day off and you will finish the day. This means that you will be able to write your own declarations, write your own prayers, and still have a section to reflect. This will allow the remainder of the book to be personalized for where you are and what you need.

I encourage you to write your declarations down as well as say them out loud to activate the confession that you are making to the Father. Let's yield today!

YIELD
DEVOTIONAL

Day One: I Yield to Your Counsel

A privilege that has become a curse to many of us is our hearing. Hearing goes beyond sound waves and just being aware of sound. Hearing is a gate, an opening, and an entire way. And even though we use this sense without thought, we have abused it without thought. Many of us have and will encounter places where answers are scarce, direction is unknown, and assurances are falsified. Therefore we seek for others to give us some kind of advise, guidance, or assurance. We open our ear-gate to those that we trust, or those whom our confidence resides. The ones who we are assured their voice, presences, and time will aid this uncomfortable place. We open ourselves to hear what we are to do just wanting the waters of our life to settle. Not knowing that just because something is a comfort to us may not be a comfort to our path.

Hearing. What voices have advised us into greater places of destruction? What voices have guided us into settling for comfort and not enduring for promise? Our ear gate has been open to sounds, phrases, verbiage, which has taken shape and form in our lives, growing legs and feet walking into our confidence, speaking into our destinies. Yes, they are just words until they are put together and form sentences that becomes our life sentence. The places and the people we open up ourselves to and exchange our current challenge/oppositions to, is more than just a sounding board, they become our life board. Some of you might be thinking I have no one whom I share with, nor anyone to talk to, but you must know you have someone whom you exchange with too, its yourself.

For some of us our own counsel is more dangerous then inviting others into that space. We get into exchanges with ourselves that cheat us out of the opportunity to see things beyond our current vantage point. I suggest that the only time we should take counsel of our own-selves is when we are listening to the voice of God. And even in that it is still good to have someone we can share these things with that only has one interest in us and that is to see us prosper. Community is important when perusing something that is greater than you. The community you surround yourself around is vital when wanting to see The Father manifest His purpose in your life. Let us yield to God's counsel and those He has called to be our community. Let's yield together.

SCRIPTURES

Psalms 73:24
Thou shalt guide me with thy counsel,
and afterward receive me to glory.

Psalms 119:24
Thy testimonies also are my delight
and my counsellors.

Psalms 16:7-8
I will bless the Lord, who hath given me counsel:
my reins also instruct me in the night seasons.
I have set the Lord always before me:
because he is at my right hand, I shall not be moved.

Ephesians 1:11-12
In whom also we have obtained an inheritance, being predestinated according to the purpose of him who worketh all things after the counsel of his own will: That we should be to the praise of his glory, who first trusted in Christ.

Isaiah 30:1-2
Woe to the rebellious children, saith the Lord,
that take counsel, but not of me;
and that cover with a covering, but not of my spirit,
that they may add sin to sin:
That walk to go down into Egypt,
and have not asked at my mouth;
to strengthen themselves in the strength of Pharaoh,
and to trust in the shadow of Egypt!

Proverbs 1:23-25
Turn you at my reproof:
behold, I will pour out my spirit unto you,

I will make known my words unto you.
Because I have called, and ye refused;
I have stretched out my hand, and no man regarded;
But ye have set at nought all my counsel,
and would none of my reproof:

Proverbs 15:22
Without counsel purposes are disappointed:
but in the multitude of counsellors they are established.

Proverbs 19:20-21
Hear counsel, and receive instruction,
that thou mayest be wise in thy latter end.
There are many devices in a man's heart;
nevertheless the counsel of the Lord, that shall stand.

Judges 18:5-6
And they said unto him, Ask counsel, we pray thee, of God, that we may know whether our way which we go shall be prosperous. And the priest said unto them, Go in peace: before the Lord is your way wherein ye go.

2 Samuel 2:1
And it came to pass after this, that David enquired of the Lord, saying, Shall I go up into any of the cities of Judah? And the Lord said unto him, Go up. And David said, Whither shall I go up? And he said, Unto Hebron.

2 Samuel 5:19
And David enquired of the Lord, saying, Shall I go up to the Philistines? wilt thou deliver them into mine hand? And the Lord said unto David, Go up: for I will doubtless deliver the Philistines into thine hand.

1 Samuel 10:22- *(Not asking For Gods counsel)*
Therefore they enquired of the Lord further, if the man should yet come thither. And the Lord answered, Behold, he hath hid himself among the stuff.

DECLARATIONS

1. I yield my ear only to the voice of the Lord
2. I close my ear gate to any other voice that has not been ordained by the Father
3. I release myself from falsified words that come from areas of my: past, failures, traumas, hurts, and alliances.
4. I declare my ear is clear of voices of condemnation, accusations, failure, demonic influences, torment, death, and destruction
5. I declare the Word of the Lord has guarded my ear gate.
6. I will adhere to the counsel of God
7. I will war over the prophetic word that comes by counsel
8. I will only seek counsel from the righteous
9. The counsel of God is enough and true concerning me.
10. I declare that I am release from word of abuse that will seek to contaminate my ear gate.
11. I declare I am release from the obligations in my relationships of hearing gossip, slander, word curses, complaining, murmuring, ungodly counsel, desires of the flesh, conspiracy and words of hatred.
12. I declare I am free from the pressure of having to know the future and its content, I embrace that Christ in me is the hope of Glory.
13. I declare that I no longer see things from my natural eye but I am seated together with Christ in heavenly places.
14. I declare I have the vantage point of heaven.
15. I declare my ears are sealed from accepting words of bought, fear, helplessness, loneliness, defeat, distraction, and desperation.

16. I declare I can hear the voice of the Lord.
17. I declare all voice that will seek to distract me from the voice of The Lord shall be silenced.
18. I declare I shall manifest all that God has ordained by ways of counsel.
19. I declare counsel shall spare me from alternate routes, ditches, holes, prisons, traps, entanglement, setback, delays, regret, missed opportunity, frustration, stolen goods, pain, discouragement, lack of direction, lack of movement, my own judgment and will, depressive state due to failure and disappointment, dissatisfaction, and despair.
20. I declare I will inquire The Lord in all things.
21. I declare I will not seek counsel to hear words of my will confirmed, but I will seek counsel that God's will be made perfect in my life.
22. I declare there is nothing to small or to great that will hinder me from seeking Gods counsel.
23. I declare I will be wise in all manners of engagement because I would have consulted The Lord.
24. I declare I will have the spirit of counsel for I carry the counselor in me.
25. I declare I will not reject The Counsel of The Lord even when it requires more of me.
26. I declare my maturity will grow in adherence to the counsel of God.
27. I declare I am divorced from all wicked consultation.
28. I declare my destiny is safe for I have the counsel of The Lord.
29. I declare I will not be afraid to stand, trust, and rely on the counsel of God.
30. I declare I yield my life only to the counsel of The Lord.

Prayer

Father, I thank you that You are God and God alone.
You are the creator of the universe and all that it contains.
High and exalted One and this day I acknowledge You.
Father I pray let Your will be done in my life.
Unto us You gave us a name that is above every name; by which, every knee must bow and every tongue must confess. By that name I have received salvation and have obtained mercy in Your sight.
And by the name You have given us power over all things.
It is by that name and that authority I pray:
IN THE NAME OF JESUS, I yield to Your counsel.
I break every alliance and agreement with wicked and familiar counsel.
I pray that my ear gate be cleansed of all vain and idol words that didn't come from You.
I adhere to Your warning according to Isaiah 30; I shall not be a child of rebellion.
I will take counsel and it shall be from the Lord and those that are God possessed.
I declare I shall only be covered with the covering of Your spirit and blood and not with the spirit of men. Father I thank you that you have protected me from my foot slipping into the downfall of my own error.
And even as I pray, I thank You that I shall be guided with the counsel of The Lord according to Psalms 73:24.
I rejoice and give You praise that even in my night season You will instruct me and give me counsel even in my ruins, as it is declared in Psalms 16:7-8.
I shall set the Lord before me always. I repent for putting the voices of others before You. I repent and come out of agreement with needing the approval of the voices of men who lack direction or themselves. I accept this day that You are a sufficient counselor, I dare not look to another.

Even as I advance in prayer, I thank you Lord! My purposes shall not be disappointed, for The Lord has given me His counsel according to Proverbs 15:22.

Father I give you praise, for You have established me in the company of counselors- spiritual advisors, prophets that bare the true voice of God, leaders that walk in wisdom and integrality, that my purposes might be established.

I revive all places of destiny that died due to ill counsel of jealousy and hatred.

I abort all present counsel whether from my own soul or others that were not ordained by You. I accept this day that You are my counselor. I dare not look to another. I yield all that I am to Your counsel.

Amen.

REFLECTIONS

Day Two: I Yield to Your Leadership

Every person and everything that was ever created on the face of this earth was created with purpose. Locked in every individual that you see daily has the purpose of God in them, and directly connected to that purpose is a path in which you can obtain the destiny of God. It's easy to walk around saying God has a plan for you but you never yield to the path and purpose of God to see that plan actualized. The only way to walk in the path is to have obtained the direction of God. Many of us have allowed life to determine what season we are in, creating demonic cycles and encircling circumstances because we lack the direction of God. When you have the direction of God, it is the divine acknowledgement as God as leader. Proverbs 3:6 say, " In all thy ways acknowledge Him, and He shall direct thy path." This verse is very clear you must first acknowledge Him.

When the Holy Spirit is leader there is no movement that takes place unless commanded by The Holy Spirit. There are business, dreams, hopes, restorations, purposes that remain in you because you lack yielded acknowledgement to He, The Holy Ghost. He wants to bring you to that expected end, but you are still commander of your life affairs. We think because we have walked with God or know His voice that He will speak when needed not understanding that the direction of God are for sons that have willingly yielding themselves. Knowing that this call and this purpose cannot be fulfilled if not led by God's spirit. This is the day of acknowledgement. That purpose, destiny, call, and path will no longer be hidden, locked, stopped nor covered any longer. Because this day, whether you been say many years or just got saved yesterday, you will make a choice that TODAY I will acknowledge You in ALL THINGS. Let's yield together.

SCRIPTURES

Psalms 23:2-3
He maketh me to lie down in green pastures: he leadeth me beside the still waters. 3. He restoreth my soul: he leadeth me in the paths of righteousness for his name's sake.

Proverbs 3:6
In all thy ways acknowledge him,
and he shall direct thy paths.

Psalms 17:5
Hold up my goings in thy paths,
that my footsteps slip not.

Isaiah 26:7
The way of the just is uprightness: thou, most upright, dost weigh the path of the just.

Jeremiah 6:16
Thus saith the Lord, Stand ye in the ways, and see, and ask for the old paths, where is the good way, and walk therein, and ye shall find rest for your souls. But they said, We will not walk therein.

Psalms 25:10
All the paths of the Lord are mercy and truth unto such as keep his covenant and his testimonies.

Psalms 119:105
NUN Thy word is a lamp unto my feet,
and a light unto my path.

Proverbs 4:18:
But the path of the just is as the shining light, that shineth more and more unto the perfect day.

Psalms 25:4-5
Shew me thy ways, O Lord; teach me thy paths. 5. Lead me in thy truth, and teach me: for thou art the God of my salvation; on thee do I wait all the day.

DECLARATIONS

1. I yield to the leadership of the Lord
2. I yield only to the direction of God
3. I yield my soul to the unction of The Holy Spirit
4. I divorce all alliances with generational curse of miss guided steps
5. I expire all familiar paths into soul activity and conversation
6. I release myself from fears of failure and I accept the spirit of faith in God.
7. I will inquire the Lord in times of not knowing and lack of guidance.
8. The Lord is my Leader and I submit my way to Him
9. I will walk in the path of the righteous
10. My sets have been order by the Lord.
11. I disengage in secret acts that cause me to walk in the path of the unjust.
12. The Lord is a lamp unto my feet and a light unto my path
13. The Lord will lead me into all truth and Godliness
14. I put my complete faith and trust in the direction of the Lord
15. I will avoid every detour to my destiny and purpose
16. I will rely completely on Gods will for my life. Even when I cannot trace nor fine His leading
17. I declare my path is straight before me.
18. I declare the leading of God will keep me from danger
19. I declare I will no longer lack directions concerning my life and destiny.
20. I declare The Lord shall teach me His path that I might walk in the ways of The Lord.
21. I declare I shall walk in a good way.
22. I declare Christ's Leadership shall expose all paths

that are hidden from my sight.
23. I declare ancient paths shall be open to me.
24. I declare power has been given to me that I might walk in new paths.
25. I declare Your word shall be a lamp unto my feet and a light unto my path.
26. I declare my foot will not slip in the path of The Lord
27. I declare mercy and truth shall be my path.
28. I declare my ways have been merged only with the way of God.
29. I declare The Lord directs my path and I shall keep that way.
30. I declare my members are yielded to Gods Leadership.

Prayer

Father, I thank you that You are God and God alone.
You are the creator of the universe and all that it contains.
High and exalted One and this day I acknowledge You.
Father I pray let Your will be done in my life.
Unto us You gave us a name that is above every name; by which, every knee must bow, and every tongue must confess. By that name, I have received salvation and have obtained mercy in Your sight.
And by the name You have given us power over all things.
It is by that name and that authority I pray:
IN THE NAME OF JESUS, I yield to your leadership
I prayer according to
Proverbs 3:6 In all thy ways acknowledge Him; and He shall direct they path. Father, I have sanctified this time in acknowledgment of You. May You govern my way and my attention focused on You and You alone. I disengage in acknowledgement of all other external powers that seek to divert my attention from You. I prophesy the Lord directs my path. I break all powers and agreements that seek to direct me outside of the counsel of the Lord. I yield, by the power of prayer, my path to You. And Father by the power of Your word in Psalms 17:5 You will hold up my goings in thy paths, that my footsteps slip not. As I yield, I declare my footsteps will not slip. For the slippery path is for the wicked and unjust. As I yield, may the slippery path be far from me this day IN JESUS NAME! I pray that You lead me in the path of righteousness for Your namesake according to Psalms 23:3. I renounce all paths of wickedness, darkness, torment, hatred, rejection, pain, and deceitfulness. My path is righteous. This day I hold to the truths of thy word. For thy word is a lamp unto my feet and a light unto my path according to Psalms 119:105. My path shall be enlighten by the light and power of they word. Even now according to Psalms 25:4-5 Shew me

thy ways, O Lord; teach me thy paths- Father, I pray, my the paths of righteousness be taught to me by the world and Spirit. Lead me in thy truth, and teach me- I declare you will teach me the way. May my soul be governed by Your truth O God. For thou art He God of my salvation; on thee do I wait all the day. Father this day I yield to your leadership.
Amen.

REFLECTIONS

Day Three: I Yield to Your Direction

There are two different types of postures you can stand in as a son. One being a son whom the Lord has revealed certain arrival point you will reach in Gods destiny for you or; you're the son that's waiting for the revealing of Gods destiny. Either way, an essential tool is required for both of these postures- divine insight. We must ask in acknowledgement that God is a God of eternity. Everything he releases he releases from the place of His eternity. This being said if we are to fulfill the destiny that the Lord has predestined for us we must know how to engage with eternity and walk in divine fulfillment.

Many of us whether we know the plan of God or have started to pursue the prize of the high calling, we need Gods instructions to reach and conceive the plans of God. Romans 8:14 declares: *For as many are led by the spirit of God they are the sons of God.* The leading of the Holy Spirit is that place of divine insight that comes from eternity, enabling us with instructions. When a vessel is seeking to fulfill the will of God life has a way of bringing situations to hinder your path, but it is the Holy Spirit who will come and give you divine insight by His leading that will direct your path. There are no roadblocks, no snares, no entanglements, and no tricks that the enemy can deploy that you cannot overcome by yielding yourself to the Holy Spirit's direction. Let's yield together!

SCRIPTURES

Psalms 32:8
I will instruct thee and teach thee in the way which thou shalt go:
I will guide thee with mine eye.

Jeremiah 33:3
Call unto me, and I will answer thee, and shew thee great and mighty things, which thou knowest not.

1 Kings 17:4
And it shall be, that thou shalt drink of the brook; and I have commanded the ravens to feed thee there.

Psalms 37:24
Though he fall, he shall not be utterly cast down:
for the Lord upholdeth him with his hand.

Joshua 1:2-3
Moses my servant is dead; now therefore arise, go over this Jordan, thou, and all this people, unto the land which I do give to them, even to the children of Israel. Every place that the sole of your foot shall tread upon, that have I given unto you, as I said unto Moses.

Genesis 12:1
Now the Lord had said unto Abram, Get thee out of thy country, and from thy kindred, and from thy father's house, unto a land that I will shew thee:

Psalms 5:8
Lead me, O Lord, in thy righteousness because of mine enemies;
make thy way straight before my face.

Psalms 27:11
Teach me thy way, O Lord, and lead me in a plain path, because of mine enemies.

Psalms 31:3
For thou art my rock and my fortress;
therefore for thy name's sake lead me, and guide me.

Psalms 86:11
Teach me thy way, O Lord; I will walk in thy truth:
unite my heart to fear thy name.

Declarations

1. I declare I yield my direction to Christ
2. I declare The Lord is my guide
3. I declare my life moves are under the influence of Christ and Christ alone
4. I declare the Holy Spirit manages my way and directs me into new places of power, peace, performance, platforms, and promotion.
5. I declare my life is under the supervision of The Holy One.
6. I declare that Christ and Christ alone will regulate every part of my being.
7. I declare my soul is governed by Gods spirit.
8. I declare my peace has been found in the direction of the Holy Spirit.
9. I declare this day and in the days to come: I will be compelled by the influence of Holy Spirit.
10. I declare my safety has been found in the will of the Father.
11. I declare my soul has been divorced from all wondering ways that will entangle me in mischief and bondage.
12. I declare my attitude has matured to a place of obedience. I this day renounce all forms for rebellion.
13. I declare all the members of my soul are submitted to the rule of the Holy Spirit.
14. I declare I will no longer walk in the way of the wicked not in their counsel concerning my path and destiny.
15. I declare my postures will be stayed and unmovable concerning the will of my Father for my destiny.
16. I declare I am in the hands of God. He holds me.
17. I declare I am confident in the leading of the Holy Spirit.

18. I declare my ears are prone to the orders and direction of The Lord.
19. I declare the prescription has been giving for all things concerning my life and destiny and that is Gods direction.
20. I declare my mind is free from distractions that will seek to hinder my direction.
21. I declare my aim has been set and will remain that which The Lord has declared from my life.
22. I declare my memory will hold and adhere to the direction of God. I will not make plans nor influence myself into alternate routes due to lack of retain that that I heard.
23. I declare all matters concerning me have been handled for The Lord directs my path.
24. I declare I lack no direction in my life for The Lord directs my path.
25. I declare I am free from failure and disappointment for my course has been fortified.
26. I declare I will arrive at divine destinations.
27. I declare I am lead by the Holy Spirit alone
28. I declare direction will be a blanket of peace when my way seems unsure.
29. I declare I will not abort direction due to difficulty
30. I declare I yield my direction to Christ.

Prayer

Father, I thank you that You are God and God alone.
You are the creator of the universe and all that it contains.
High and exalted One and this day I acknowledge You.
Father I pray let Your will be done in my life. Unto us You gave us a name that is above every name; by which, every knee must bow, and every tongue must confess. By that name, I have received salvation and have obtained mercy in Your sight. And by the name You have given us power over all things. It is by that name and that authority I pray:
IN THE NAME OF JESUS, I yield to Your direction.

    Father, even as I pray I thank You that You have untied my heart in reverence of Your name, that You may teach me the ways of Your path according to Psalms 86:11. I will walk in Your way. I speak that I am free from the way of the wicked and the unrighteous. For thou art my rock and my fortress, I find my safety in You and You alone. You shall guide me and lead me for they name sake according to Psalms 31:3. And God even as You lead me I thank You that You shall lead me into places of provision and surplus in times of drought and famine. Even as You did for Your servant The Prophet- You lead him to a brook:

    I thank You that You shall lead me to the brooks of refreshing, brooks of revival, brooks of increase, brooks of opportunities, brooks of Godly success, brooks of dreams, brook of vision, brooks of encounter, brooks of glory, and brooks of breakthrough. And even as I pray, You command a raven- a birth that was selfish to feed him. I thank You that ravens shall be commanded to feed me because the Holy Spirit is my director. Father may this word be established by 1 Kings 17:4 Even as You did it for Your servant the prophet LET IT BE UNTO ME THIS DAY. By thy spirit and by the authority of the word I pray this prayer. This day I yield to Your direction. Amen.

REFLECTIONS

Day Four: I Yield to Your Strength

Strength goes way beyond our physical ability. In my observation through my tenure of ministry, I have noticed that our strength level most times is determined by our mental state. When the mind says that we our weak our body comes into agreement with it. When our mind says we are strong the body follows and so on, but the key is strength must be built in the minds of our spirits more so than our natural minds. What is a spiritual mind? The mind is no longer in you it is in Christ Jesus. You have been renewed in your mind and have taken on the mind of Christ (Phil. 2:5)- His thinking, His understanding, His paradigm.

As I yield my level of consciousness to God, Holy Spirit, and His Word, strength becomes available. Reading the word of God should be more than an obligation. You should purposefully read God word and pray knowing that when I do these things I gain strength. I obtain an advantage every time I posture the word and myself in the place of prayer. *Jude 1:20 But ye, beloved, building up yourselves on your most holy faith, praying in the Holy Ghost.*

First, we must acknowledge that there are diabolical powers that want to tear you DOWN. These powers begin to attach to your possessions, your health, your progress, and your goals and once the assault has been made, our minds carry the brunt of the impact. However, we have been assured and this confidence has been given unto us that we build up ourselves unto holy faith, praying in the Holy Ghost. This coupling of the word and prayer aids the places we lack strength. Let's yield together.

Myself, I Give, Willingly

SCRIPTURES

Psalms 46:1
To the chief Musician for the sons of Korah, A Song upon Alamoth.
God is our refuge and strength,
a very present help in trouble.

Proverbs 18:10
The name of the Lord is a strong tower:
the righteous runneth into it, and is safe.

Nehemiah 8:10
Then he said unto them, Go your way, eat the fat, and drink the sweet, and send portions unto them for whom nothing is prepared: for this day is holy unto our Lord: neither be ye sorry; for the joy of the Lord is your strength.

Philippians 4:13
I can do all things through Christ which strengtheneth me.

Isaiah 40:29
He giveth power to the faint;
and to them that have no might he increaseth strength.

Psalms 119:28
My soul melteth for heaviness:
strengthen thou me according unto thy word.

Ephesians 6:10
Finally, my brethren, be strong in the Lord, and in the power of his might.

Isaiah 40:31
But they that wait upon the Lord shall renew their strength;
they shall mount up with wings as eagles;
they shall run, and not be weary;
and they shall walk, and not faint.

Psalms 22:19
But be not thou far from me, O Lord:
O my strength, haste thee to help me.

Psalms 118:14
The Lord is my strength and song,
and is become my salvation.

Isaiah 33:2
O Lord, be gracious unto us; we have waited for thee:
be thou their arm every morning,
our salvation also in the time of trouble.

Habakkuk 3:19
The Lord God is my strength,
and he will make my feet like hinds' feet,
and he will make me to walk upon mine high places.
To the chief singer on my stringed instruments

DECLARATIONS

1. I declare I have the strength of God
2. I declare in my weakness Gods strength is made perfect
3. I declare and renounce all weariness that will come to stop my acceleration.
4. I declare my strength is in knowing that God is with me and will not forsake me.
5. I declare the strength of God will be enforced in every weak place of my life.
6. I declare the bravery to blazes new trails to the glory of God.
7. I declare strength to overcome sickness, death, pain, and hardship.
8. I declare strength to carry out new vision to its completion.
9. I declare the backbone to stand against demonic influences of generational curses, regional principalities, and governmental oppression.
10. I declare I have the force to break barriers, bust through gates of opposition, and prevail ambush and attack.
11. I declare I will not allow natural circumstances to drain me of virtue.
12. I declare my emotional state is strength during times of warfare.
13. I declare this day and the days to come that my strength is in Christ and Christ alone.
14. I declare new strength in praying, fasting, seeking, dwelling, understanding, and new mysteries of the Spirit.
15. I declare all areas of my life that I have given my strength in vain- may those doors be closed! Never to open again less they are in their appointed time.

16. I declare strength to face the mountains and valleys of life.
17. I declare durability as I run this race of patience. I will not be worn out.
18. I declare power to arise in my spirit.
19. I declare divine advantage over systems and streams of influence The Lord has called me to.
20. I declare all limitations of my power have been broken
21. I declare I will grow in the grace of my power
22. I declare may I be magnified in Christ, the one who makes me a thousand times more.
23. I declare I will make sound decisions in my life and ministry
24. I declare resilience in the pursuit of my destiny.
25. I declare depth and favor in my spiritual understanding of Gods truth and word.
26. I declare supernatural skill in my gifts and talents. For they are The Lords.
27. I declare advantage in my career and professional reputation.
28. I declare I will no longer run due to resistances that have been built to discourage my course. For my muscle has been built to breakthrough resistance.
29. I declare I have the courage of a soldier fighting on the frontline. I will not be afraid of arrows nor the sound of war. For the Lord has given me victory.
30. I declare I have the strength of God.

PRAYER

Father, I thank You that You are God and God alone.
You are the creator of the universe and all that it contains.
High and exalted one and this day I acknowledge You.
Father I pray let Your will be done in my life.
Unto us You gave us a name that is above every name; by which, every knee must bow and every tongue must confess. By that name I have received salvation and have obtained mercy in Your sight.
And by the name You have given us power over all things.
It is by that name and that authority I pray:
IN THE NAME OF JESUS, I yield to Your strength.
Father, I thank You that You are my strength and You cause me to walk in high places according to Habakkuk 3:19
And even as Your strength is made perfect for me that I might rise to high places and walk- be not far from me Lord. For You are my strength, hear my cry and hasten to help me.
God, I also thank You in times of hardship, pressure, and obscurity that Your name shall become a strong tower for me- and this day I run into Your name- Jehovah- Jireh the Lord shall provide, Jehovah- Rapha the Lord who Heals, Jehovah-Nissi the Lord my banner, Jehovah- M'kaddesh the Lord who sanctifies and makes Holy, Jehovah- Tsidkenu the Lord my righteousness, Jehovah- Shammah the Lord is there, I run into Your name.
Father I pray this prayer by Your spirit and the authority of the word.
I yield to Your strength.
Amen.

REFLECTIONS

Day Five: I Yield to Your Lordship

When we give our lives to Christ, many times it is really just a surrendering of our hearts and not a life give away. We discussed this in our open introduction; however, I want us to further explore this thought. Even though we gave our lives to Him, we still experience difficulties, challenges, addictions, and life tolerances that are not pleasing to The Lord. Yes, we all have a process to sanctification, but many of us have not experienced true freedom because God only occupies the name and place of Savior and not Lord. We treat God like a resource and not like He is the source of all. Certain areas of our life are still under our control; therefore, we have roped off and limited His love from reaching those places. Lordship means dominion, authority, rank, territory under a jurisdiction. He wants full control and authority of our lives.

Full control can be a hard thing to comprehend for a lot of us being that this place is unknown to us. But let me give you a new vantage point. When you yield to Gods Lordship, it is no longer your responsibility to fix, handle, or take care of these places. It's now in the hands of Abba to give you the tools and directions to freedom. Now if you don't adhere to the instructions and commands of God than who is still in command? Yielding disciplines the members of your body to come into agreement with the Father's will for your life.

I'm not saying that you don't play a role in bettering yourself, however, many of us are playing the wrong role. You want to put yourself under anesthesia and be the doctor that operates on yourself. It doesn't work. We must stop trying to fix ourselves and allow Holy Spirit to compete the work that He started in us. Relieve yourself of that pressure that comes from religion and live your life responsible in grace. It is not your job to fix anything about you or your life; it is your job to yield to the desire and intent of your doctor-your Father. Let's yield together!

SCRIPTURES

Galatians 5:1
Stand fast therefore in the liberty wherewith Christ hath made us free, and be not entangled again with the yoke of bondage.

James 4:7
Submit yourselves therefore to God. Resist the devil, and he will flee from you.

Psalms 32:7
Thou art my hiding place; thou shalt preserve me from trouble; thou shalt compass me about with songs of deliverance. Selah.

Psalms 34:17
The righteous cry, and the Lord heareth,and delivereth them out of all their troubles.

1 John 5:4
For whatsoever is born of God overcometh the world: and this is the victory that overcometh the world, even our faith.

I Peter 5:8-9
Be sober, be vigilant; because your adversary the devil, as a roaring lion, walketh about, seeking whom he may devour: Whom resist stedfast in the faith, knowing that the same afflictions are accomplished in your brethren that are in the world.

2 Samuel 22:2
And he said, The Lord is my rock, and my fortress, and my deliverer;

Romans 6:14
For sin shall not have dominion over you: for ye are not under the law, but under grace.

DECLARATIONS

1. I yield to the Lordship of Christ
2. I declare my soul is kept by God
3. I declare I am released from the leadership of governing myself without the instruction of Christ my Lord
4. I declare the Lord is the Bishop of my soul
5. I declare I am the clay and The Lord is my potter- He has made me.
6. I declare the members of my soul is under the command of Christ my Lord
7. I declare Christ and Christ alone rules over me
8. I declare my soul is free from old covenants of dominion
9. I repent of all forms of idolatry knowingly and unknowingly
10. I declare, in this present time, I renounce all fear from yielding my soul to the Lord
11. I declare I shall be in complete compliance with the Lordship of Christ
12. I declare Christ created me therefore He has rule over me
13. I declare I will have deliverance for my soul
14. I declare the Lord is my deliverer- sin shall not bring me to shame
15. I declare all powers of rebellion, haughtiness, stubbornness, and pride will not have power over me for the Lord is my deliverer.
16. I declare I am free from the responsibility of freeing myself. For I am do nothing on my own- Christ is my deliverer.
17. I declare that grace has empowered me and the law has been broken off of me.
18. I declare my soul is free from all dominion of sin

19. I declare that God has built in me the will power to resist the devil that he might flee from me in the time of temptation, hardship, difficulty, storms of life, trouble, transition, elevation, waiting, breakthrough, success, and visibility.
20. I declare that I am steadfast and unmovable
21. I declare Christ has made me free who can bind me
22. I declare may my eye see the yoke of bondage that comes to trap me in former and familiar sins of the past.
23. I declare my desire for the yoke the Lord has delivered me from is broken
24. I declare my mind has been cover by Christ's blood- therefore my thoughts are free
25. I declare I have the mind of Christ
26. I declare I am sober
27. I declare The Lord is my hiding place
28. I declare I am preserved from trouble
29. I declare The Lord is the keeper of my soul
30. I declare my soul is yielded to the Lordship of Christ

PRAYER

Father, I thank You that You are God and God alone.
You are the creator of the universe and all that it contains.
High and exalted One and this day I acknowledge You.
Father I pray let Your will be done in my life.
Unto us You gave us a name that is above every name; by which, every knee must bow, and every tongue must confess. By that name, I have received salvation and have obtained mercy in Your sight.
And by the name You have given us power over all things.
It is by that name and that authority I pray:
IN THE NAME OF JESUS, I yield to Your Lordship.
And even as I pray I thank You that sin no longer has dominion over me.
For I have been freed from the law and I am now under grace according to romans 6:14.
And even as I pray I thank You that You have delivered me from the yoke of bondage, death, sin, oppression, and demonic influences. And as I advance in prayer I am assured that when I cry You will heal me and delivery me out of all my afflictions according to Psalms 34:17. You are my hiding place.
I find my safety in You, peace in You, hope in You, joy in You, all that I need in You, for You have preserved me from trouble.
This day I relieve myself of the care to deliver myself, and I yield to Gods deliverance.
Father, I pray this prayer by the spirit and the authority of the word.
Amen.

REFLECTIONS

Day Six: I Yield to Your Lordship Pt. 2

One of the first things that I noticed when I moved out of the house at seventeen and got my first apartment was that I didn't own much. Though furnishing my first apartment was enjoyable for me, at times, what made it most exciting was that everything in my apartment was mine! I worked for it, paid for it, and owned it. Therefore, when others would come over there were certain rules that you had to follow. This was not a means to control anyone however; I instituted these rules in protection of my investment. I valued what the Lord had graced me to acquire.

See, you are God's "first apartment", and the gifts and calling of God are the possessions He owns, yes, even your life. When Jesus paid the price for you it was not you choosing Him, it was Him choosing you- He hand picked you and despite Him paying with His life He still doesn't have full control over what He paid for. Just as He chose you, He wants you to choose Him back. Praise is the act of us openly choosing the father back. You can live your life in constant praise when you willing lay your life down even as Christ laid His life down for us.

God wants complete dominance over all that concerns you; where your only will is to please Him. Everything that was created was made for the pleasure of God and everything that was created was created for His glory. But when man fell into sin the whole world was made subject to vanity. In turn, man choosing the one who loves them above all things rectifies this vanity. Submit yourself this day unto the Spirit of the Lord- yield, that Christ might be glorified in you. When God only has the title, role, and position as savior in your life and is not The Lord, your soul is left open to the things of your past. These yokes begin to grow and become stronger because the savior saves your soul, but when He's the Lord He DELIVERS and KEEPS it. When He's Lord you open yourself to experience the penetrating power of His love. It knows no boundaries or any power greater than itself. Yield that He might be Lord! Let's yield together.

SCRIPTURES

Psalms 82:8
Arise, O God, judge the earth: for thou shalt inherit all nations.

Leviticus 20:26
And ye shall be holy unto me: for I the Lord am holy, and have severed you from other people, that ye should be mine.

Isaiah 43:1
But now thus saith the Lord that created thee, O Jacob,
and he that formed thee, O Israel,
Fear not: for I have redeemed thee,
I have called thee by thy name; thou art mine.

Zechariah 2:12
And the Lord shall inherit Judah his portion in the holy land, and shall choose Jerusalem again.

Psalms 6:4
Return, O Lord, deliver my soul:
oh save me for thy mercies' sake.

Psalms 116:4
Then called I upon the name of the Lord;
O Lord, I beseech thee, deliver my soul.

Psalms 121:7
The Lord shall preserve thee from all evil:
he shall preserve thy soul.

Psalms 56:13
For thou hast delivered my soul from death: wilt not thou deliver my feet from falling,
that I may walk before God in the light of the living?

DECLARATIONS

1. I declare, The Lord is the Lord and keeper of my soul
2. I declare my trust is in the Lord to deliver my soul
3. I declare all parts of my life are submitted under the dominance of the Father.
4. I declare my soul shall be delivered
5. I declare this day, all past, and present alliances that has been formed to challenge my submission to God shall be broken and destroyed
6. I declare the hand of The Lord shall cover me from paths not ordained by God
7. I declare all secret, hidden, and unknown idols that would seek to exalt themselves in my life shall be broken down. Even as you broke down the god of Dagon.
8. I declare my soul has submitted itself unto the truths of Gods word and spirit
9. I declare it is The Lord that I look to, no other shall capture my soul
10. I declare The Lord shall save my soul in times of trouble, adversity, and hardship. lack, pain, and difficulty.
11. I declare The Lord is the keeper of my soul
12. I declare my soul shall only be kept by The Lord
13. I declare may all soul contaminants be purified by the fire of God
14. I declare my body is the temple of The Holy Ghost
15. I declare my life shall be preserved because The Lord is my keeper
16. I declare The Lord is my shepherd I shall not want
17. I declare when I call upon The Lord He shall deliver me
18. I declare my soul shall be an inheritance for Christ's death

19. I declare when my enemies come to devourer my soul they shall be utterly destroyed by the one who keeps my soul
20. I declare all soul-ish cycles the keep my emotions, memory, time, economy, success, exits and entries trapped is now broken by the strong arm of the Lord
21. I declare all powers that come to negatively influence the will of my soul have been reversed and resisted by the help of God.
22. I declare I have been redeemed by God, for He keeps my soul
23. I declare I am kept by God
24. I declare all powers of rejection, shame, condemnation that speaks to the gates of my soul shall be silenced by the love of my Father
25. I declare I am The Lord's sheep and I only hear His voice
26. I declare strength to not open myself to familiar powers, people, systems, and tactics that seek the destruction of my soul.
27. I declare power to resist soul temptation
28. I declare I shall be holy unto the Lord
29. I declare that it shall be my souls delight to serve the Lord
30. I declare my soul is kept by God

PRAYER

Father, I thank You that You are God and God alone.
You are the creator of the universe and all that it contains.
High and exalted One and this day I acknowledge You.
Father, I pray, that Your will be done in my life.
Unto us, You gave us a name that is above every name; by which, every knee must bow, and every tongue must confess.
By that name, I have received salvation and have obtained mercy in your sight.
And by the name You have given us power over all things.
It is by that name and that authority I pray:
IN THE NAME OF JESUS, I yield to Your Lordship.
And by Your mercies shall my soul be saved.
I thank You Lord that You have made covenant with me by Your word and according to Leviticus 20:26 that I shall be holy for You are holy.
And this day I accept that You have severed me from all that I might be Yours.
I bring my soul into agree with Your word, that I am Yours and You are mine.
And Father I further thank You that when times of adversity comes to put my soul in aguish You shall deliver me when I call, according to Psalms 116:4
And You won't just hear me but You will also deliver me.
This day I comply! The Lord is the keeper of my soul and no other shall have me.
Father, I pray this prayer by the spirit and the authority of the word.
Amen.

REFLECTIONS

Day Seven: I Yield to Your Protection

Every day we are faced with many circumstances, whether good or bad, that demands our attention and ultimately a reply must be given. Most of us however have structured ourselves to believe that things come to us in the nature in which we need to respond to them in. For an example, if an event occurs in our life that is tragic, we respond with the appropriate behavior or emotion. Despite this truth, every natural response doesn't always mean a Godly response. As life continues to bring its trouble, even as it was declared that a man born of a women is a few days and full of trouble (Job 14:1) we must acquire the appropriate approach when facing this trouble if we expect to get Godly results. One of the main areas we need this in is protection. When these powers of the world come to suppress your destiny, kill your passions, and stifle your success it take the protection of God to defend you.

The enemy comes by approaching us with the issues of life to provoke the parts of us that are dead; all in the efforts of tugging a response out of us that defiles us and makes his accusations true concerning the former us. Hosts called people carry out most times these assignments of hell! People at your work establishments, people at your institutions of education, and people closest to you; all designed to get a responds out of you that either forfeits your place or resurrects the you that is dead. We must gain the Godly understanding that even though its people that are causing trouble in my life these warrants were initiated by hell.

Furthermore, if these things are issued in the spirit realm it will take a spiritual response to counter the attack that was warranted. You are God's and in you He put good things, things called His treasure. And if God will give His son for you and pay a price for you what makes you think He won't protect what He bankrupted heaven for? When these things come, your response should be to God and allow Him to respond to those things. Yield to God's protection that the enemies of your life, destiny, and family be scattered at His upraising. Let's yield together!

SCRIPTURES

2 Thessalonians 3:3
But the Lord is faithful, who shall establish you, and keep you from evil.

Deuteronomy 31:6
Be strong and of a good courage, fear not, nor be afraid of them: for the Lord thy God, he it is that doth go with thee; he will not fail thee, nor forsake thee.

Isaiah 41:10
Fear thou not; for I am with thee: be not dismayed; for I am thy God: I will strengthen thee; yea, I will help thee; yea, I will uphold thee with the right hand of my righteousness.

Proverbs 4:6
Forsake her not, and she shall preserve thee: love her, and she shall keep thee.

Psalms 5:11
But let all those that put their trust in thee rejoice: let them ever shout for joy, because thou defend them: let them also that love thy name be joyful in thee.

Psalms 20:1
The Lord hears thee in the day of trouble; the name of the God of Jacob defend thee;

Psalms 46:1
God is our refuge and strength, a very present help in trouble.

Psalms 138:7
Though I walk in the midst of trouble, thou wilt revive me:

thou shalt stretch forth thine hand against the wrath of mine enemies, and thy right hand shall save me.

Psalms 140:4
Keep me, O Lord, from the hands of the wicked; preserve me from the violent man; who have purposed to overthrow my goings.

Psalms 91:1
He that dwelleth in the secret place of the most High shall abide under the shadow of the Almighty.

DECLARATIONS

1. I declare I yield myself to God's protection
2. I declare all response that raise in me by ungodly provoking shall be overtaking by God's righteousness
3. I declare The Lord shall keep me in divine protection
4. I declare when I call The Lord in trouble He shall rescue me
5. I declare The Lord shall keep me from the hands of the wicked
6. I declare the wicked shall fall before me when they seek to destroy my going in and coming out
7. I declare I shall abide under the shadow of the almighty, for He is my protector
8. I declare The Lord shall preserve me from violent men
9. I declare in the mist of wicked men you shall revive me
10. I declare your hand shall be against those that seek to assault me
11. I declare The Lord shall hear me in the day of trouble
12. I declare The Lord of Host shall raise to my defense when the host of this world come to attack my purpose, destiny, health, family, strength, success, economy, favor, name, places of authority, and places of influence
13. I declare the protection of God shall be upon those that I love
14. I declare all powers of the world that come to cause tragedy in my family, life, and career shall be destroyed by God fire
15. I declare The Lord shall protect my name from all forms of accusation whether spiritual, verbal or written

16. I declare my destiny has been fortified by the defense of God
17. I declare that God will release angelic assistance to defend His causes in my life and ministry
18. I declare The Lord shall teach my hands to war and my fingers to fight
19. I declare The Lord shall be my peace in the mist of those that want to see me fall
20. I declare may the way of the wicked be slippery lest they repent
21. I declare divine exposure to those that prize me publicly but seek by down fall in private
22. I declare I shall be strong and of a good courage
23. I declare The Lord shall help me and uphold me with His right hand
24. I declare all fear and man pleasing spirit that raise in me are taken out of me by way of thee anointing
25. I declare God shall be my refuge in the time of trouble
26. I declare the name of the Lord is my strong tower I run in it and I am safe
27. I declare who is the world against me when God is for me
28. I declare The Lord has given me the victory over mine enemies
29. I declare the victory of The Lord shall be stayed in my house
30. I declare I yield to God's protection

PRAYER

Father, I thank You that You are God and God alone.
You are the creator of the universe and all that it contains.
High and exalted One and this day I acknowledge You.
Father, I pray, let Your will be done in my life.
Unto us, You gave us a name that is above every name; by which, every knee must bow and every tongue must confess. By that name, I have received salvation and have obtained mercy in Your sight.
And by the name You have given us power over all things.
It is by that name and that authority I pray:
IN THE NAME OF JESUS, I yield to Your protection.
Father I thank You that Psalms 20:1 is activated over my life
For You shall hear me in the day of trouble and defend me from those that seek my demise.
Father this day, I declare that You shall keep me from the hands of the wicked and preserve me from the violent one.
You shall rise to my defense for I turn to You and You alone.
I thank You that You shall teach me the way of righteousness and the members of my soul shall stand in agreement with Your word.
For You declared Isaiah 41:10 Fear thou not; I thank You that fear has no place in my life
For I am with thee: I thank You that You are with me and You will not forsake me be not dismayed; for I am thy God: Father I stand in the assurance that You are God and besides You there is no other
I will strengthen thee; yea, I will help thee; I prophesy now that Your strength shall be upon me and Your help this day I receive
yea, I will uphold thee with the right hand of my righteousness. And Father I thank You that You shall uphold me in all things. In Jesus' name Amen!

Reflections

Day Eight: I Yield to Your Truth and Word

The ENEMY has one major power he using against the believer, he speak to them. Though this may be hard to receive, the enemy speaks to you to plant words (which are seeds) in your heart in order to get you to abort the word that the Father has spoken over you. This very thing he did to Eve in the Garden. He was able to get her to conceive something other than what God had spoken to them. The danger is every thing the enemy speaks is a LIE even when it seems to be the TRUTH. NO! Let me declare it again. EVERYTHING THE DEVIL SPEAKS TO YOU IS A LIE.

When you open yourself to reason with words other than what God has spoken your life it has the potential to submit itself to a lie. There is no such thing as half the truth. Either it is the truth or it is a lie. Anything that starts true but ends in fabrication is still made up. As a believer, you no longer live under the accusations of the enemy. The Lord said the thoughts He thinks towards you are of good and not of evil. He longs to see you fulfill all that He has spoken over you, however we open ourselves to the lies of the enemy.

The Word of God is not a book of stories, its a book of prophesy for you and your families life. When we yield ourselves to the word of God, we are excepting God's truth about our life, community, society, and the like. Religion tells us that we have to go through the prayer line, purge in a bucket, role on the floor, and mess up our cloths to be free. Now, corporate deliverance is essential and eternal, however cooperate deliverance means nothing if your heart doesn't except what God thinks and has predestined over your life. You have prayed and prayed for certain behaviors, challenges, and tolerances to be removed from your life yet they are still there. Why? Know this, these things don't live in you they live in your understanding, which is your truth. To be renewed in your mind is to be renewed in your truth. Yielding yourself to God's word and truth brings a level of deliverance and freedom that provokes peace and the joy of the Lord in your life. Let's yield together!

SCRIPTURES

Psalms 119:142
Thy righteousness is an everlasting righteousness, and thy law is the truth.

Psalms 119:43
And take not the word of truth utterly out of my mouth; for I have hoped in thy judgments.

Psalms 119:160
Thy word is true from the beginning: and every one of thy righteous judgments endureth for ever.

2 Corinthians 6:7
By the word of truth, by the power of God, by the armour of righteousness on the right hand and on the left,

Matthew 22:16
And they sent out unto him their disciples with the Herodians, saying, Master, we know that thou art true, and teachest the way of God in truth, neither carest thou for any man: for thou regardest not the person of men.

Galatians 2:5
To whom we gave place by subjection, no, not for an hour; that the truth of the gospel might continue with you.

Ephesians 1:13
In whom ye also trusted, after that ye heard the word of truth, the gospel of your salvation: in whom also after that ye believed, ye were sealed with that holy Spirit of promise,

2 Timothy 3:16
All scripture is given by inspiration of God, and is profitable for doctrine, for reproof, for correction, for instruction in righteousness:

John 17:17
Sanctify them through thy truth: thy word is truth.

1 John 2:8
Again, a new commandment I write unto you, which thing is true in him and in you: because the darkness is past, and the true light now shineth.

DECLARATIONS

1. I declare I yield to God's truth and word
2. I declare all soul-ish powers that come to push me from God's truth and word shall be broken in Jesus name
3. I declare I listen and obey no other voice but the voice of the Father
4. I declare my trust and faith shall be placed in the truth of Gods word
5. I declare I shall be planted on the sure foundation which is The Word of God
6. I declare Your word is my doctrine, my reproof, and my instructions of righteousness
7. I declare I shall hear the word of truth and stand in its power
8. I declare all lies spoken by false doctrine, false teachers, and false prophets shall fall to the ground and die in my life and in the life of those I love
9. I declare nothing shall separate me from the truth of Your word
10. I declare I shall be sanctified in truth
11. I declare all spirits of rebellion that want to operate in me and in my life against Your word shall be judged and broken by fire
12. I declare I shall find delight in obeying the truth of Your word
13. I declare I shall walk in the light of Your word Oh Lord
14. I declare the truth of the gospel shall remain with me
15. I declare I shall subject myself to the truth of Your word
16. I declare I shall testify of Your word
17. I declare my life shall reflect and resemble the truth of Your word

18. I declare may You open my understanding of Your word
19. I declare all darkness of disorder, lack of understand, and carnality shall be removed from my life
20. I declare Your word shall bring light at the entrance of it in my life
21. I declare by Your Spirit shall You teach me Your word and to do it
22. I declare Your truth is the law of my life
23. I declare the word that I utter shall be Your truth as I wait on Your direction
24. I declare my tongue shall be sanctified from all lies knowingly and unknowingly
25. I declare Your judgments in my life are true
26. I declare the sum of Your words are true
27. I declare my mind shall retain the words of Your truth
28. I declare all ideologies, theories, and mysticism shall die in my life and in those that I love
29. I declare You shall not take the words of truth out of my mouth
30. I declare I yield to your truth and word

PRAYER

Father, I thank You that you are God and God alone.
You are the creator of the universe and all that it contains.
High and exalted One and this day I acknowledge You.
Father, I pray, let Your will be done in my life.
Unto us, You gave us a name that is above every name; by which, every knee must bow, and every tongue must confess. By that name, I have received salvation and have obtained mercy in Your sight.
And by the name You have given us power over all things.
It is by that name and that authority I pray:
IN THE NAME OF JESUS, I yield to Your truth and word.
Even this day I stand on the faith and believe that Your righteousness is everlasting and Your law is truth.
Father, I pray may the lies of the enemies of my soul be uprooted and be put far from me.
For I shall walk in the law of Your truth and my life shall be submitted under that law of truth.
And I pray even according to Psalms 119:43 do not take the word of truth utterly out of my mouth, for I wait for Your ordinances.
Even as I pray I declare may the words of truth be stayed in my mouth, that I might declare Your truth long as I live. For I look and wait for Your direction, mandate and order. This day I submit myself to the truth of Your word knowing that all of Your words are true for me.
This day I renounce all forms of lies spoken to me either by the error of men or things that I've spoken over myself in ignorance. I pray according to John 17:17 Sanctify them in the truth Your words are truth. I thank You that as You sanctified them in Your truth You will sanctify me. Let that portion be upon me and those in my humanity. In the name of Jesus, Amen

REFLECTIONS

DAY NINE: I YIELD TO YOUR FORGIVENESS

One of the most powerful skills we have learned is memory. We depend on this motor function in our everyday life. We are continually keeping record of events that happen in our day-to-day lives but some events that occur have the capacity to stain our memories. These stains become engrafted into our heart and who we are. Most times, even if we do not remember all of the events that led up to that moment we hold to the effects of the occurrence. Can you imagine that even though time has continued we have taken memories and memorialized them? When we don't yield and forgive, we take those moments and keep living in a time that no longer exists! These moments only exist in you. Un-forgiveness traps you in a time that only lives because you have memorialized a moment. When the pain, unsettled, deformed, regretful, and mistakes of our life still has the effect attached to them they carry the power to mold the current with something that happened formerly. Yielding yourself to forgiveness opens your life up to release you from the effect of the memory and moments, that you might settle those times in your life.

Most people that have un-forgiveness in their lives have a hard time accepting and believing that God has forgiven them. And even if they know that He has forgiven them, they still look for a punishment or some type of give and take to settle the score not understanding that God's forgiveness is perfect and not like men. It's not a question of whether you love God or not, the problem is we don't love ourselves enough to except His love that causes Him to forgive us. We bind ourselves to our failures even after repentance. We must accept first, God's forgiveness of us and when we do that we cannot but help to forgive others. Mercy is given to those that give mercy. Yield, that the effect of your pain, traumas, falls, and failures can be removed into complete freedom in Christ. Here's a reminder that can help you with the process of forgiveness. Let's just simply look at the word, for-give. You must release those things that were *be-fore* and *give* your now to God; that's the true state of forgiveness. To be in a place where you have released yourself from before so you can give God your NOW! Let's yield today!

SCRIPTURES

1 John 1:9
If we confess our sins, he is faithful and just to forgive us our sins, and to cleanse us from all unrighteousness.

Colossians 3:13
Forbearing one another, and forgiving one another, if any man have a quarrel against any: even as Christ forgave you, so also do ye.

Matthew 6:14
For if ye forgive men their trespasses, your heavenly Father will also forgive you:

Luke 13:3
I tell you, Nay: but, except ye repent, ye shall all likewise perish.

Ephesians 4:32
And be ye kind one to another, tenderhearted, forgiving one another, even as God for Christ's sake hath forgiven you.

Proverbs 24:29
Say not, I will do so to him as he hath done to me: I will render to the man according to his work.

Proverbs 25:21
If thine enemy be hungry, give him bread to eat; and if he be thirsty, give him water to drink:

Matthew 5:7
Blessed are the merciful: for they shall obtain mercy.

Matthew 6:12
And forgive us our debts, as we forgive our debtors

DECLARATIONS

ACCEPTING CHRIST'S FORGIVENESS:

1. I declare my soul is yielded to forgiveness
2. I declare my acceptance of God's forgiveness for me
3. I declare all past mistakes, traumas, failures, and offences that will seek to imprison me in un-forgiveness, I am released from them all NOW
4. I declare all covenants I have made with old places, dead places, wasted, places, and cripple places to aid my pain are renounced this day
5. I declare all insecurities that form in my soul to keep me from forgiving myself and accepting Christ's forgiveness are broken now
6. I declare all doors of shame, valley's of shame, and realms of shame that came by way of sin and unrighteousness are renounced this day
7. I declare all entries of sin that manifest through hosts whether in people, places, or things that seek to bring shame upon my name, my family, my ministry, my anointing, and my manifestation are now broken by Christ's blood
8. I declare my acceptance of God's forgiveness for me
9. I declare that God has forgiven me of all my sins and transgressions
10. I declare God's love for me
11. I declare even the things Christ doesn't want in me He has a love for them-He chastises them
12. I declare Christ's forgiveness is forever
13. I declare all powers of deceit that come to mask my present reality and acknowledgement of sin is broken by Christ's blood
14. I declare my flesh shall submit to Christ's spirit and confess my faults, without fear

15. I declare as I confess my faults the Lord shall forgive me and remember them no more

RELEASING CHRIST'S FORGIVENESS:
16. I declare all people and places that is or have offended me are release from my soul, emotions, and remembrance whether knowingly or unknowingly
17. I declare any fault that I am holding against my brothers and sisters in the Lord have been released this day
18. I declare the love of the Lord shall help me in times of offence
19. I declare The Lord shall teach me how to forgive that the heavenly Father might forgive me
20. I declare forgiveness will be easy for me
21. I declare that I will consider others over myself
22. I declare my heart is guarded from offence
23. I declare I forgive quickly and love eternally
24. I declare any pregnancies against by brothers or sisters that I have or will be held in my heart are broken by Christ power
25. I declare I will pray for my brothers and sisters when they confess their faults to me that we both might be healed
26. I declare I will have the spirit of boldness to go to those that have offended me that we may both reconcile in love
27. I declare Christ's heart of forgiveness shall become my heart of forgiveness
28. I declare The Lord shall help me forgive others even as He has forgiven me
29. I declare I shall be kind even if I am not being treated kind and loving even if I am not being treated lovingly, and The Lord shall give me the spirit of wisdom in transitioning relationship that have forfeited Christ covenant
30. I declare I have Christ's forgiveness

PRAYER

Father, I thank You that You are God and God alone.
You are the creator of the universe and all that it contains.
High and exalted One and this day I acknowledge You.
Father, I pray, let Your will be done in my life.
Unto us, You gave us a name that is above every name; by which, every knee must bow, and every tongue must confess. By that name I have received salvation and have obtained mercy in Your sight.
And by the name You have given us power over all things.
It is by that name and that authority I pray:
IN THE NAME OF JESUS, I yield to Your forgiveness.
I release myself from all those that have gained the title of offender on my life
And I forgive them even as You have forgiven me according to Colossians 3:13.
Father, as I pray I prophesy may I grow in love, mercy, and compassion for those that I have held to their offences. This day, in prayer, I ask that You forgive me for holding any of my brothers or sisters in knowingly and unknowingly. Father, I rid myself of all bitterness and the sting of the pains and failures of my past. I thank You that as I forgive my offenders You will forgive me according to Luke 17:3 and 4.
Father I thank You that Your word declares that if I confess my sins, You will be faithful and just. You will forgive my sins and purify me from all unrighteousness.
I ask this day that I be purified in all righteousness.
In Jesus' name, Amen.

REFLECTIONS

Day Ten: I Yield to Your Joy

We live in a time where there are constant pressures that want to weigh us down. Being a believer there will be times that our faith is challenged by life's current presentation. In turn, the enemy begins to present to you your present to weaken your faith of your promise. Clear signs of this assault manifests in our emotions and stamina to prevail to the place of destiny. When strength is lost whether it is mental, physical and or spiritual we open ourselves to understandings and truths that didn't come from the Father.

Joy is not just feeling good, joy is a weapon of war that acts as a garrison between you and the enemy. Intentionally living in joy doesn't mean that everything in our life will be well. Living in joy provokes our life to wellness. God's joy is your strength, aiding you into a place of breakthrough and sustaining you while you wait on them. Let yield today.

SCRIPTURES

1 Thessalonians 5:16-18- ^{16}Rejoice evermore. ^{17}Pray without ceasing ^{18}In every thing give thanks: for this is the will of God in Christ Jesus concerning you.

Psalms 118:24- This is the day, which the Lord hath made; we will rejoice and be glad in it.

John 16:24- Hitherto have ye asked noting in my name: ask, and ye shall receive, that your joy may be filled.

1 Timothy 6:6- But godliness with contentment is great gain.

Hebrews 11:6- But without faith it is impossible to please him: for he that cometh to God must believe that he is, and that h is a rewarder of them that diligently seek him.

Proverbs 12:20- Deceit is in the heart of them that imagine evil: but to the counselors of peace is joy.

Philippians 4:4- Rejoice in the Lord always: and again, I say, Rejoice.

Psalm 16:11- Thou wilt shew me the path of life: in thy presence is fullness of joy; at thy right hand, there are pleasures for evermore.

Proverbs 15:23- A man hath joy by the answer of his mouth: and a word spoken in due season, how good is it!

DECLARATIONS

1. I declare I have the joy of The Lord
2. I declare The Lord is my strength
3. I declare The Lord strengthens me with joy
4. I declare joy shall be in my house
5. I declare joy shall be my shield against frustration, anger, rage, hopelessness, fear, regret, anxiety, and emotional distress
6. I declare my life shall be full of the goodness of God
7. I declare I shall drink from the fountains of joy
8. I declare I shall be a source of joy for others to encounter
9. I declare I will have joy even when I'm waiting for God's understanding in my life
10. I declare joy shall overflow in my life
11. I declare all enemies of my joy shall be exposed and dismantled by God's fire
12. I declare I will give thanks to The Lord in all things, and joy shall be the fruit of my thanksgiving
13. I declare the reward of my journey is receiving the more of The Lord, therefore I shall have joy
14. I declare The Lord is the defender, keeper, infuser, and sustainer of my joy
15. I declare this day that I will rejoice in the Lord.
16. _____
17. _____
18. _____
19. _____
20. _____
21. _____
22. _____
23. _____
24. _____

25. _____
26. _____
27. _____
28. _____
29. _____
30. _____

Prayer

Father, I thank you that You are God and God alone.
You are the creator of the universe and all that it contains.
High and exalted One and this day I acknowledge You.
Father, I pray, let Your will be done in my life.
Unto us, You gave us a name that is above every name; by which, every knee must bow, and every tongue must confess. By that name I have received salvation and have obtained mercy in Your sight.
And by the name You have given us power over all things.
It is by that name and that authority I pray:
IN THE NAME OF JESUS, I yield to Your joy.

Stokes International

REFLECTIONS

Day Eleven: I Yield to Your Timing

When I was a child, I had a tuned ear for a certain sounds that would echo throughout our neighborhood. It was the sound of the ice cream truck. I was able to tell you how many blocks away he was and if he was coming in our direction or not. When I saw the truck stop either near or afar from me, I would bolt to it, but my mother would always be there demanding that I wait. WAIT? I have been waiting on this ice cream truck all day and you want me to wait? I would get so frustrated and anxious I would exhaust myself. What's the important of this? I wanted to go ahead of my mother never realizing I had no provision for what I could see ahead of me. A life not yielded to the timing of God will cause frustration, anxiety, fear, contentment, and most of all failure.

God doesn't reveal our destinies to us to make us ambitious. He shows us them to set our hearts on the prize of His high calling, to entice your heart into the understanding that His thoughts and plans about you are good and not evil. We are to be a people that are not ambitious but anointed. When the anointing is on you, it's on you for a certain time. However you cannot miss that time when you are in Gods timing. The era or moment will put a demand for you and your anointing. The enemy always come to make us feel like we have missed our time or as if time is not moving fast enough, but with God being a God of time it's assured that even if your time is stolen, taken, missed, or breeched God has the power to restore your time. Let's yield today.

SCRIPTURES

Psalms 27:14 - Wait on the LORD: be of good courage, and he shall strengthen thine heart: wait, I say, on the LORD.

Habakkuk 2:3 - For the vision [is] yet for an appointed time, but at the end it shall speak, and not lie: though it tarry, wait for it; because it will surely come, it will not tarry.

Psalms 62:5 - My soul, wait thou only upon God; for my expectation [is] from him.

Isaiah 40:31 - But they that wait upon the LORD shall renew [their] strength; they shall mount up with wings as eagles; they shall run, and not be weary; [and] they shall walk, and not faint.

Psalms 130:5 - I wait for the LORD, my soul doth wait, and in his word do I hope.

Proverbs 3:5-6 – ⁵ Trust in the LORD with all thine heart; and lean not unto thine own understanding. ⁶ In all thy ways acknowledge him, and he shall direct thy path

Galatians 6:9 - And let us not be weary in well doing: for in due season we shall reap, if we faint not.

Lamentations 3:25-26 - ²⁵The LORD [is] good unto them that wait for him, to the soul [that] seeketh him. ²⁶ [It is] good that [a man] should both hope and quietly wait for the salvation of the Lord.

Micah 7:7 - Therefore I will look unto the LORD; I will wait for the God of my salvation: my God will hear me.

DECLARATIONS

1. I declare I yield my life to God's timing
2. I declare my strength shall be renewed in my waiting
3. I declare that my life's steps are syncopated with Gods divine plan for my life
4. I declare God's timing is perfect in all things
5. I declare my soul will not be anxious for anything causing me to enter in to premature time
6. I declare I will not move outside of God's timing due to life pressures, my own understandings, and my own reasoning
7. I declare all words that my time has past and will be no more are broken
8. I declare all powers that come to stall my time, steal my time, kill my time, restrict my time, limit my time, replace my time are broken by the power of The Holy Spirit
9. I declare my idle time shall be full of the purposes of God and His Kingdom
10. I declare all powers that will provoke the down fall of my time will not withstand in the hour of my revealing
11. I declare all former season that seek to intervene with my present time and future time are destroyed to be no more
12. I declare I have been graced to transition from time to time, season to season, and grace to grace by God's Spirit
13. I declare opportunities that were mishandle by my own deeds or the works of others have been redeem by Christ's blood
14. I declare my only vantage point of time is that which has been given by heaven and not my emotions
15. I declare God's timing over my life

16. _____
17. _____
18. _____
19. _____
20. _____
21. _____
22. _____
23. _____
24. _____
25. _____
26. _____
27. _____
28. _____
29. _____
30. _____

Prayer

Father, I thank You that You are God and God alone.
You are the creator of the universe and all that it contains.
High and exalted One and this day I acknowledge You.
Father, I pray, let Your will be done in my life.
Unto us, You gave us a name that is above every name; by which, every knee must bow, and every tongue must confess. By that name, I have received salvation and have obtained mercy in Your sight.
And by the name You have given us power over all things.
It is by that name and that authority I pray:
IN THE NAME OF JESUS, I yield to your timing.

REFLECTIONS

Day Twelve: I Yield to Your Holiness

Religion has taken the messages of holiness and instituted legalistic laws to imprison and ensnare God's people in constant condemnation. These legalistic laws imprison and ensnare the people of God by establishing rules and protocols that set a standard many cannot and will never reach. This kind of legalistic or "Godly living" will push God's church to accept the world's view and force God out of the church instead of setting a standard of holiness that allows the church to keep God as the focus of daily living. Holiness is a scary word in this generation. It has cause grace to be insufficient. We have made God far from us instead of near to us. Holiness is not the lens that reveals your imperfections and flaws to make you feel worthless and less than. Holiness is the reflection of God in his people.

He wants to see you without spot or blemish. Looking and reflecting Him in all that you do. Holiness is the acknowledgement that God is holy therefore I am. I'm going to write it again. Holiness is the acknowledgement that God is holy therefore I am. Holiness is not looking at you then comparing yourself to a perfect God. Holiness is looking at the Father and yielding to the understanding that He is I and I am He. Let's yield today.

SCRIPTURES

1 Thessalonians 4:7 - For God hath not called us unto uncleanness, but unto holiness.

1 Thessalonians 5:23 - And the very God of peace sanctify you wholly; and [I pray God] your whole spirit and soul and body be preserved blameless unto the coming of our Lord Jesus Christ.

1 Peter 2:9 - But ye [are] a chosen generation, a royal priesthood, an holy nation, a peculiar people; that ye should shew forth the praises of him who hath called you out of darkness into his marvelous light:

Hebrews 12:14 - Follow peace with all [men], and holiness, without which no man shall see the Lord:

2 Corinthians 7:1 - Having therefore these promises, dearly beloved, let us cleanse ourselves from all filthiness of the flesh and spirit, perfecting holiness in the fear of God.

1 Peter 1:15-16 — [15]But as he which hath called you is holy, so be ye holy in all manner of conversation; [16]because it is written, Be ye holy; for I am holy

Romans 12:1 – I beseech you therefore, brethren, by the mercies of God, that ye present your bodies a living sacrifice, holy, acceptable unto God, which is your reasonable service.

1 Samuel 2:2- There is none holy as the Lord: for there is none beside thee: neither is there any rock like our God.

Leviticus 20:26- And ye shall be holy unto me: for I the Lord am holy, and have severed you from other people, that ye should be mine.

DECLARATIONS

1. I declare I am holy for The Lord is Holy
2. I declare all forms of self condemnation from others, systems, and myself have been broken off of my life
3. I declare Christ in me shall perfect my soul
4. I declare holiness is obtainable
5. I declare I accept the doctrine of Christ Holiness
6. I declare I shall see myself as Christ sees me
7. I declare all alliances that will compromise my pursuit of holiness is destroyed by Christ's blood
8. I declare all spirits of torment that come to keep me in a place of shame have been released from my soul
9. I declare holiness is Christ manifesting in me
10. I declare I am a reflection of Christ's holiness for others to see
11. I declare The Lord shall help me where I am weak that I might be better
12. I declare in my weakness Christ strength will be made perfect
13. I declare The Lord shall help me in the places I willingly compromise
14. I declare holiness shall be in all parts of my life
15. I declare I will live a holy life
16. _____
17. _____
18. _____
19. _____
20. _____
21. _____
22. _____
23. _____
24. _____
25. _____
26. _____

27. _____
28. _____
29. _____

PRAYER

Father, I thank You that You are God and God alone.
You are the creator of the universe and all that it contains.
High and exalted one and this day I acknowledge You.
Father, I pray, let Your will be done in my life.
Unto us, You gave us a name that is above every name; by which, every knee must bow, and every tongue must confess. By that name, I have received salvation and have obtained mercy in Your sight.
And by the name You have given us power over all things.
It is by that name and that authority I pray:
IN THE NAME OF JESUS, I yield to Your holiness.

REFLECTIONS

Day Thirteen: I Yield to Your Fathering

Mary the mother of Jesus was only thirteen when the angle came to her that day and told her she would conceive by the overshadowing of the Holy Ghost. She wasn't just young; she was engaged to be married. How freighting could it have been for Mary, that there was a possibility that her soon to be spouse will reject her. The Lord had to speak to Joseph to settle his understanding. However, in all of this, Mary and Joseph was just the avenue, the channel to fulfill the prophesy of the savior's coming. We live our lives based on the families we are born in and not the one that sent us to our families.

Whether your childhood was great or not so great the grace of God is made perfect for us when God manifests Himself as Father. In the beginning, God creates the heavens and earth, now making Him the originator of all things. In this, God was not just this deity that demands our worship and our praise; He is a Father that has prepared this place for His sons and daughters that they might know Him and display His nature. Allow God to be your Father. Give Him the permission to become a source/ originator of everything in your life. No matter how old or young you are He longs to be Father, the source of all that you need. Let's yield today.

SCRIPTURES

Proverbs 20:7 - The just [man] walketh in his integrity: his children [are] blessed after him.

Proverbs 13:24 - He that spareth his rod hateth his son: but he that loveth him chasteneth him betimes.

3 John 1:4 - I have no greater joy than to hear that my children walk in truth.

Proverbs 3:11-12 - [11]My son, despise not the chastening of the LORD; neither be weary of his correction: [12] For whom the LORD loveth he correcteth; even as a father the son [in whom] he delighteth.

Ephesians 1:5 - Having predestinated us unto the adoption of children by Jesus Christ to himself, according to the good pleasure of his will,

Psalms 27:10 - When my father and my mother forsake me, then the LORD will take me up.

Romans 8:14- For as many as are led by the Spirit of God, they are the sons of God.

Romans 8:15 -For ye have not received the spirit of bondage again to fear; but ye have received the Spirit of adoption, whereby we cry, Abba, Father.

Romans 8:16-17- [16]The sprit itself beareth witness with our spirit, that we are the children of God: [17] and if children, then heirs; heirs of God, and joint-heirs with Christ; if so be that we suffer with [him], that we may be also glorified together.

DECLARATIONS

1. I declare I yield to The Lord being my Father
2. I declare I no longer have the spirit of an orphan for I have been adopted into a royal family.
3. I declare rejection has no place in my life because my Father has accepted me just as I am
4. I declare I will not live my life only to see God's demands and not His love
5. I declare The Lord shall father me into the vessel He wants me to be
6. I declare I have a Father who loves me. He is my heavenly Father
7. I declare I shall come unto The Lord as a little child
8. I declare The Fathers love is perfect for me
9. I declare all soul wombs that will keep my soul from receiving Christ as Father have been removed
10. I declare The Lord shall raise me in all things pertaining to Godliness and His Kingdom because He is my Father
11. I declare every area of my life shall be fathered by The Lord
12. I declare I will not be limited by generational curses, for I have been adopted into a royal family
13. I declare my soul is at rest in the care of my Father
14. I declare the Lord is the start of all things in my life. He motivates my choices, decisions, actions, direction, and movement.
15. I declare The Lord is my Father
16. _____
17. _____
18. _____
19. _____
20. _____
21. _____

22. _____
23. _____
24. _____
25. _____
26. _____
27. _____
28. _____
29. _____
30. _____

PRAYER

Father, I thank You that You are God and God alone.
You are the creator of the universe and all that it contains.
High and exalted One and this day I acknowledge You.
Father, I pray, let Your will be done in my life.
Unto us, You gave us a name that is above every name; by which, every knee must bow, and every tongue must confess. By that name, I have received salvation and have obtained mercy in Your sight.
And by the name You have given us power over all things.
It is by that name and that authority I pray:
IN THE NAME OF JESUS, I yield to Your fathering.

REFLECTIONS

Day Fourteen: I Yield to Your Spirit

When Saul went in search of his fathers donkeys in 1 Samuel 10 you will find that he came to the prophets house and the prophet begins to prepare him for something he was not even in search for. Upon Saul leaving, Samuel gave him some instructions concerning what he would see and what he must do upon leaving. These set of instructions included him coming to a company for prophets that was coming down from a high place. When he met this company of prophets the Bible declares that the Spirit of the Lord came upon him and he began to prophesy and was turned into another man. This is just one of the accounts in the Bible where the Spirit of God can come upon someone and give them a divine ability that they didn't have before.

Was Saul a prophet? NO. He was anointed to be king, however, being in the company of those prophets the spirit of prophecy came upon him. The spirit of God comes to do more then just give us physical manifestations that we can feel. He comes to led us in the path of righteousness, comfort us, protect us, give us counsel, and most of all show fourth God nature in us. You will be constantly faced with things that seem bigger than you. Most times until we accept our calling, it too seems bigger than us. But we are not met to fulfill these things in our own ability we are called to do then in the spirit of God. This life is not about living a full life. It's about living a life poured out because it's full of the spirit. God is looking for those He can show fourth His glory through and manifest His nature in. Just as Saul did when you yield to God's spirit watch Him change you into another man. Let's yield today.

SCRIPTURES

Galatians 5:22-23- ²²But the fruit of the Spirit is love, joy, peace, longsuffering, gentleness, goodness, faith, ²³Meekness, temperance: against such there is no law.

John 4:24- God is a Spirit: and they that worship him must worship him in spirit and in truth

Isaiah 61:1- The Spirit of the Lord God is upon me; because the Lord hath anointed me to preach good tidings unto the meek; he hath sent me to bind up the brokenhearted, to proclaim liberty to the captives, and the opening of the prison to them that are bound.

Psalms 51:10- Create in me a clean heart, O God; and renew a right spirit within me

John 3:6- That which is born of the flesh is flesh; and that which is born of the Spirit is spirit.

2 Corinthians 3:17- Now the Lord is that Spirit; and where the Spirit of the Lord is, there is liberty.

Luke 4:18- The Spirit of the Lord is upon me, because he hath anointed me to preach the gospel to the poor; he hath sent me to heal the brokenhearted, to preach deliverance to the captives, and recovering of sight to the blind, to set at liberty them that are bruised.

1 Peter 1:13- Wherefore gird up the loins of your mind, be sober, and hope to the end for the grace that is to be brought unto you at the revelation of Jesus Christ.

Galatians 5:16- This I say then, walk in the Spirit, and ye shall not fulfill the lust of the flesh

Galatians 5:25- If we live in the Spirit, let us also walk in the Spirit.

DECLARATIONS

1. I declare I have the spirit of God
2. I declare I will not resist God's spirit from using me in all that I do
3. I declare the spirit of God has empowered me to do all things
4. I declare by God's spirit I shall overcome every obstacles that invades my path with difficulty and hardship
5. I declare God's spirit rules my life and the direction thereof
6. I declare I am not afraid to boldly walk in the spirit of God
7. I declare I am a son of God therefore I have the spirit of God
8. I declare I lack no comfort for God's spirit shall be my comforter
9. I declare I lack no wisdom for God's spirit shall teach me all things
10. I declare By God's spirit I shall access realms of revelation and divine insight
11. I declare I will be a activator of God's nature everywhere I go
12. I declare God's spirit shall overtake me when spirits of angry, rage, pain, misunderstanding, retaliation, regret, torment, frustration, and agony come to invade my spirit
13. I declare my spirit has yielded to Christ spirit
14. I declare there is no other spirit I have but Christ spirit living in me
15. I declare I yield to the spirit of God
16. _____
17. _____
18. _____

19. _____
20. _____
21. _____
22. _____
23. _____
24. _____
25. _____
26. _____
27. _____
28. _____
29. _____
30. _____

Prayer

Father, I thank You that You are God and God alone.
You are the creator of the universe and all that it contains.
High and exalted One and this day I acknowledge You.
Father, I pray, let Your will be done in my life.
Unto us, You gave us a name that is above every name; by which, every knee must bow, and every tongue must confess. By that name, I have received salvation and have obtained mercy in Your sight.
And by the name you have given us power over all things.
It is by that name and that authority I pray:
IN THE NAME OF JESUS, I yield to Your spirit.

REFLECTIONS

Day Fifteen: I Yield to Your Grace

Normality becomes the prison of a Christian that has yoked themselves to societies standards. Everyone is not the same and that's okay. We have built systems that scream when anyone decides to break the mold or do something different. Even though we are in one of the most innovating times, we are only evolving to please and be accepted in a system we are called to change. You have a choice. Your life can either be a prison or a platform. The distinction between these two places of holding is that when your life is a prison, you have all of this promise in you and spoken over you, yet you limit yourself to your education or the job that pays the bills never reaching your true potential.

Not knowing that greater is He that's in you than He that's in the world. When your life is a platform, you lay down your life that Christ might stand on it and show His glory to all. God gives us divine abilities to aid us in the destiny He has called us to. These abilities come by God bestowing His grace upon us. Grace doesn't just save us; it empowers us. Every man is given a measure of grace and within that grace comes a power that prophesies to the present what is to come. Why be normal when you can display Gods glory? Why settle when you can reveal the Fathers heart? You're not normal you have been graced! You're not just a mom, dad, sister, brother, etc. the Almighty has graced you. His hand is on your life and you will bring Him glory. Let grace, which is that divine enabling to do something work its perfect work in your life. Let's yield today.

SCRIPTURES

2 Corinthians 12:9 - And he said unto me, My grace is sufficient for thee: for my strength is made perfect in weakness. Most gladly therefore will I rather glory in my infirmities, that the power of Christ may rest upon me.

2 Peter 3:9 - The Lord is not slack concerning his promise, as some men count slackness; but is longsuffering to us-ward, not willing that any should perish, but that all should come to repentance.

James 4:6 - But he giveth more grace. Wherefore he saith, God resisteth the proud, but giveth grace unto the humble.

1 Corinthians 15:10 - But by the grace of God I am what I am: and his grace which [was bestowed] upon me was not in vain; but I laboured more abundantly than they all: yet not I, but the grace of God which was with me.

Hebrews 4:16 - Let us therefore come boldly unto the throne of grace, that we may obtain mercy, and find grace to help in time of need.

1 Peter 5:10 - But the God of all grace, who hath called us unto his eternal glory by Christ Jesus, after that ye have suffered a while, make you perfect, stablish, strengthen, settle [you].

Ephesians 1:7 - In whom we have redemption through his blood, the forgiveness of sins, according to the riches of his grace;

2 Corinthians 9:8 - And God [is] able to make all grace abound toward you; that ye, always having all sufficiency in all [things], may abound to every good work

DECLARATIONS

1. I declare the grace of God is on my life
2. I declare divine ability has been given to me by the Father
3. I declare there is no restriction to what I can do within my measure of grace
4. I declare grace has perfected my path into great exploits
5. I declare I have been graced to accomplish my life's roles (speak your roles: father, mother, sister, co-worker, manager, team leader, pastor, leader, etc.)
6. I declare I will no longer limit myself but I will look to the Lord to reveal my measure of grace
7. I declare when I am overwhelmed I will not fret for grace has been given to me
8. I declare I will be gracious for the Lord has been gracious to me
9. I declare I will share God's grace with those in my humanity
10. I declare all normality's that seek to lock me into systems of compromise have been broken by God's power
11. I declare signs shall follow my life by virtue of me being a believer in The Lord Jesus
12. I declare all man pleasing spirit has been broken off of my life
13. I declare all pressure bestowed by the expectations of man has been removed from my shoulders. For there is only one that I seek to please and that is the Lord
14. I declare all fear has been broken of my life's assignment and life's calling
15. I declare, today that I yield to the grace of God that is on my life
16. _____

17. _____
18. _____
19. _____
20. _____
21. _____
22. _____
23. _____
24. _____
25. _____
26. _____
27. _____
28. _____
29. _____
30. _____

PRAYER

Father, I thank You that You are God and God alone.
You are the creator of the universe and all that it contains.
High and exalted One and this day I acknowledge You.
Father, I pray, let Your will be done in my life.
Unto us, You gave us a name that is above every name; by which, every knee must bow, and every tongue must confess. By that name, I have received salvation and have obtained mercy in Your sight.
And by the name You have given us power over all things.
It is by that name and that authority I pray:
IN THE NAME OF JESUS, I yield to Your grace.

REFLECTIONS

Day Sixteen: I Yield to Your Provision

We all have ideas of where we want to be and how we want to get there. Most times life has a way of constantly trying to reroute us in to constant revision of what we saw for our lives and family. Sight is just that sight. It only gives you the ability to see. However, when you have vision it speaks the purpose of why you see what you see. Vision comes to enlist us into the plan of God for our lives. Provision comes to those that have reached that place of sight with purpose. Provision is just what the word says, Pro-vision.

When God funds something, He does it with a purpose. He longs to release His resources to us yet we only want Him to provide for places that are temporal and don't speak to the place of favor and destiny the Lord has called us to. God's provision doesn't come to provide for a place He has not called, it comes to those that have yielded their sight to His purpose. God is pro His vision and He will release provision to those that will carry it. Let's yield today.

SCRIPTURES

Philippians 4:19 - But my God shall supply all your need according to his riches in glory by Christ Jesus.

Matthew 6:33 - But seek ye first the kingdom of God, and his righteousness; and all these things shall be added unto you.

Psalms 37:25-26 - I have been young, and [now] am old; yet have I not seen the righteous forsaken, nor his seed begging bread.

Matthew 6:26 - Behold the fowls of the air: for they sow not, neither do they reap, nor gather into barns; yet, your heavenly Father feedeth them. Are ye not much better than they?

Psalms 23:1 - (A Psalm of David.) The LORD [is] my shepherd; I shall not want.

Philippians 4:6 - Be careful for nothing; but in every thing by prayer and supplication with thanksgiving let your requests be made known unto God.

Jeremiah 29:11 - For I know the thoughts that I think toward you, saith the LORD, thoughts of peace, and not of evil, to give you an expected end.

Malachi 3:10 - Bring ye all the tithes into the storehouse, that there may be meat in mine house, and prove me now herewith, saith the LORD of hosts, if I will not open you the windows of heaven, and pour you out a blessing, that [there shall] not [be room] enough [to receive it].

DECLARATIONS

1. I declare that I have the provision of God
2. I declare my vision has been filled with the purpose of God
3. I declare I lack nothing for the Lord has provided me with all things
4. I declare The Lord has provided all that I need
5. I declare divine resources have been released to fulfill the purposes of God
6. I declare I shall be a good steward over that which The Lord has provided for me
7. I declare The Lord shall provide protection for transition
8. I declare the provision of God shall not lay waste due to lack of vision
9. I declare I will be faithful over few things that God might make me ruler over many
10. I declare I will be sensitive to the voice of the Lord concerning the sowing of my provision
11. I declare Kings, friends, my enemies, the just, and the unjust shall give unto my bosom
12. I declare my anointing shall be accommodated with the provisions
13. I declare I shall have provision unto an inheritance for generations to come
14. I declare provision shall be my weapon of establishment in purpose
15. I declare today I have yielded to the provisions of God
16. _____
17. _____
18. _____
19. _____
20. _____

21. _____
22. _____
23. _____
24. _____
25. _____
26. _____
27. _____
28. _____
29. _____
30. _____

Prayer

Father, I thank You that You are God and God alone.
You are the creator of the universe and all that it contains.
High and exalted One and this day I acknowledge You.
Father, I pray, let Your will be done in my life.
Unto us, You gave us a name that is above every name; by which, every knee must bow, and every tongue must confess.
By that name, I have received salvation and have obtained mercy in Your sight.
And by the name You have given us power over all things.
It is by that name and that authority I pray:
IN THE NAME OF JESUS, I yield to Your provision

Myself, I Give, Willingly

REFLECTIONS

Day Seventeen: I Yield to Your Breakthrough

Resistance! The battle ground for those that have set their hearts on movement. Resistance doesn't come to those that are not moving. Which means there is a qualification in order to met resistance in your life. Though resistance can mask itself in obstacles that seem to be impenetrable, resistance is not a bad thing. It's an indication that something has been initiated. There are some things that are not meant to be worked out, they are meant to be broken through! We must allow the breaking so we can get through to the platform of manifestation. We love to get to the side of manifestation; it is the breaking that we have a problem with. In order for the attack or plan of the enemy to be legal, he has to have a vessel. Anyone or anything can become a conduit of the devil to be used to cause resistance. The enemy uses these people or things to frustrate the movement in our lives. He wants you to get frustrated and loss your focus. He wants you exhausted so that you can lose stamina and endurance until you get to the point of break down, not breakthrough. These daily obstacles are opportunities to teach you how to handle conflict and hardship when your destiny is on the line.

Most of us seek to reach the place of our destiny not understanding that destiny is simply a destination that you first arrive to in yourself than you get to in status. Along that journey to your destiny, there are tools that the Father gives you to assist you in your initiation of something new. Breakthrough is one of those tools. It aids you when facing barriers, difficulties, strange powers, principalities, and any other form of resistance. When you yield to the breakthrough of God you don't have to fight, The Lord fights for you. In yielding, He gives you wisdom that ensures no loss. Most of all breakthroughs causes there to be a release in your life. Whatever has come to imprison you and stop you from elevation and moving forward, the power of breakthrough destroys it at contact! Let's yield today.

SCRIPTURES

Isaiah 54:17 - No weapon that is formed against thee shall prosper; and every tongue [that] shall rise against thee in judgment thou shalt condemn. This [is] the heritage of the servants of the LORD, and their righteousness [is] of me, saith the LORD.

Ephesians 6:12 - For we wrestle not against flesh and blood, but against principalities, against powers, against the rulers of the darkness of this world, against spiritual wickedness in high [places].

John 8:32 - And ye shall know the truth, and the truth shall make you free.

Acts 1:8 - But ye shall receive power, after that, the Holy Ghost is come upon you: and ye shall be witnesses unto me both in Jerusalem, and in all Judaea, and in Samaria, and unto the uttermost part of the earth.

Ephesians 3:20 - Now unto him that is able to do exceeding abundantly above all that we ask or think, according to the power that worketh in us,

Psalms 91:3- Surely he shall deliver thee from the snare of the fowler, [and] from the noisome pestilence.

Hebrews 4:12 - For the word of God [is] quick, and powerful, and sharper than any two-edged sword, piercing even to the dividing asunder of soul and spirit, and of the joints and marrow, and [is] a discerner of the thoughts and intents of the heart.

1 John 4:4 You are from God, little children, and have overcome them; because greater is He who is in you than he who is in the world.

2 Corinthians 10:3-5 [3] For though we walk in the flesh, we do not war after the flesh: [4] For the weapons of our warfare are not carnal, but mighty thought God to the pulling down of strong holds; [5] Casting down imaginations, and every high thing that exalteth itself against the knowledge of God, and bringing into captivity every thought to the obedience of Christ.

Ephesians 6: 11-17- [11] Put on the whole armour of God, that ye may be able to stand against the wiles of the devil. [12] For we wrestle not against flesh and blood, but against principalities, against powers, against the rulers of the darkness of this world, against spiritual wickedness in high places. [13] Wherefore take unto you the whole armour of God, that ye may be able to withstand in the evil day, and having done all, to stand. [14] Stand therefore, having your loins girt about with truth, and having on the breastplate of righteousness; [15] And your feet shod with the preparation of the gospel of peace; [16] Above all, taking the shield of faith, wherewith ye shall be able to quench all the fiery darts of the wicked. [17] And take the helmet of salvation, and the sword of the Spirit, which is the word of God:

DECLARATIONS

1. I declare the breakthrough of God
2. I declare in all things that seeks to hinder my path shall encounter The Lords breakthrough
3. I declare The Lord shall break me through all resistance, hindrances, obstacles, chains, hardships, oppressions, glass ceilings, boundaries, limitations, and mental blocks.
4. I declare I am not afraid for breakthrough shall find me in every valley, every drought, every mountain, and every hard place
5. I declare breakthrough shall aid me to places of great influence and promotion as The Lord wills
6. I declare the breakthrough of my hearts limitation to be broken for the things that breaks my Father's heart
7. I declare constant breakthroughs in my mercy, compassion, kindness, and love
8. I declare the breaking of The Lord shall be upon all powers that seek to see me fail
9. I declare that breakthrough is not just for me but also for those I love and am in covenant with
10. I declare breakthrough shall be upon a thousand generations after me
11. I declare breakthrough in my witness to others
12. I declare breakthrough shall never be late but come in the time it is most needed
13. I declare The Lord has taught my hands to war and my fingers to fight
14. I declare breakthrough has been made for all my businesses, assets, investments, accounts, and all things attached to my name and the establishment thereof
15. I declare today that I yield to the breakthrough of God

16. _____
17. _____
18. _____
19. _____
20. _____
21. _____
22. _____
23. _____
24. _____
25. _____
26. _____
27. _____
28. _____
29. _____
30. _____

Prayer

Father, I thank You that You are God and God alone.
You are the creator of the universe and all that it contains.
High and exalted One and this day I acknowledge You.
Father, I pray, let Your will be done in my life.
Unto us, You gave us a name that is above every name; by which, every knee must bow, and every tongue must confess. By that name, I have received salvation and have obtained mercy in Your sight.
And by the name You have given us power over all things.
It is by that name and that authority I pray:
IN THE NAME OF JESUS, I yield to Your breakthrough.

REFLECTIONS

Day Eighteen: I Yield to Your Sending

In the beginning, God spoke everything into being including who we were and the dominion and reign we would have over the Earth. He establishes in Ephesians 1 that before the foundations of the world that He choose us within Himself. God tells Jeremiah that before he was formed in his mother's womb that He already knew him. What is the importance and tie between all of these references? Your birth was not just a conclusion of your parent's actions; it was the channel of God sending you here. God sent you here as a word to all of Earth.

Isaiah 55 declares that not a word will return unto Him void. What He sent that word to do it will be fulfill. Even as Jesus the Christ was sent to the world to redeem the world, so are we sent into the world to display and show fourth His person. Jesus was the word made flesh and we should strive to embody the words of God within us. Life can be full of tasks but how much of our lives are we giving to what He sent us here to do? Has time even been invested into determine that occupation of grace? Yielding to God's sending stimulates your life to matriculate to a place of significance. Let's yield today.

SCRIPTURES

John 15:16- Ye have not chosen me, but I have chosen you, and ordained you, that ye should go and bring forth fruit, and [that] your fruit should remain; that whatsoever ye shall ask of the Father in my name, he may give it to you.

1 Peter 2:9- But ye [are] a chosen generation, a royal priesthood, an holy nation, a peculiar people; that ye should shew forth the praises of him who hath called you out of darkness into his marvelous light.

Ephesian 1:4 According as he hath chosen us in him before the foundation of the world, that we should be holy and without blame before him in love

Revelation 3:20 – Behold, I stand at the door, and knock: if any man hear my voice, and open the door, I will come in to him, and will sup with him, and he with me.

Deuteronomy 7:6- For thou art an holy people unto the Lord thy God; the Lord they God hath chosen thee to be a special people unto himself, above all people that are upon the face of the earth.

Matthew 22:14- For many are called, but few are chosen

Ephesians 2:19- Now therefore ye are no more strangers and foreigners, but fellow citizens with the saints, and of the household of God.

2 Thessalonians 2:13- But we are bound to give thanks always to God for you, brethren beloved of the Lord, because God hath from the beginning chosen you to salvation through sanctification of the Spirit and belief of the truth

Romans 8:28- And we know that all things work together for good to them that love God, to them who are the called according to his purpose.

DECLARATIONS

1. I declare I am Sent by God
2. I declare I am not here in the Earth just to be here but I have purpose
3. I declare God values me therefore He sent me
4. I declare my steps have been ordered by The Lord
5. I declare The Lord is the sole influence of my path and way and He uses those whom He has called to aid me in my journey
6. I declare the courage to walk the path The Lord has called me too
7. I declare strength to resist the ways of compromise
8. I declare I will be steadfast in the will of God
9. I declare I will walk in the fulfillment of every spoken word over my life that has been ordained by Christ, my Father
10. I declare fear will not cripple my faith in the plans of God for my life
11. I declare I have been sanctified for the sending of The Lord
12. I declare I share in the ministry of reconciliation of those that are not saved
13. I declare The Lord sent me therefore He will protect me
14. I declare I will not be afraid of the faces of those He has called me to both seen and unseen
15. I declare today that I yield to being sent by God
16. _____
17. _____
18. _____
19. _____
20. _____
21. _____
22. _____

23. _____
24. _____
25. _____
26. _____
27. _____
28. _____
29. _____
30. _____

Prayer

Father, I thank You that You are God and God alone.
You are the creator of the universe and all that it contains.
High and exalted One and this day I acknowledge You.
Father, I pray, let Your will be done in my life.
Unto us, You gave us a name that is above every name; by which, every knee must bow, and every tongue must confess. By that name, I have received salvation and have obtained mercy in Your sight.
And by the name You have given us power over all things.
It is by that name and that authority I pray:
IN THE NAME OF JESUS, I yield to Your sending.

Reflections

Day Nineteen: I Yield to Your Love

God's eternity is forever. It goes without end. He Himself is eternal. He needs no one or nothing for by Him all things were established and created. He sustains Himself. However, though He is all those things, He makes a choice to make us in His image and likeness. And He further goes to save the world because He loves it. He chooses to make His habitation in our praise. Though this is hard for the human mind to wrap around if we don't have a personal revelation of His love, we subject our lives to living a legalistic and religious life and not manifesting a relationship. The greatest power given to man is love. The greatest gift is nothing and tainted when its not maintained by love. Yielding to God's love raises our compliance to His will for our lives. The bible declares that if you love Me you will obey My commandments. This doesn't mean that if you break them or you are growing in a place to live them that you don't love God. It actually is revealing that if you grow in love with God that your obedience to God will increase. It's much easier to take instruction and correction from someone that you love than someone you feel stuck too. I don't serve Him because I don't want to go to hell. I serve Him because I love Him.

Love just doesn't help you to obey it anoints you. Love releases the kind of oil that allows spiritual gifts to flow with ease. You cannot help the one that you don't love, nor will you give your life for someone you don't care for. Love is a requirement for a believer. The word of The Lord declares how can you love the one you have not seen when you don't love the one that you see. Most times, we love and view the love of God through the lens of how we have been loved or lack thereof. No matter what your resume is, in relationships of love its certain that if you have a revelation of His love it will teach you how to love Him. There are certain thing that we have not conquered in our lives because we are trying to think them away in us instead of allow God to love them away. Yielding to God's love opens you to be completely emerged in the intent of why you have this relationship with Him, because you love Him. Let's yield today!

SCRIPTURES

1 Corinthians 13:4-5- ⁴Charity suffereth long, and is kind; charity envieth not, charity vaunteth not itself, is not puffed up, ⁵Doth not behave itself unseemly, seeketh not her own, is not easily provoked, thinketh no evil

1 Corinthians 16:14 Let all your things be done with charity.

Colossians 3:14- And above all these things put on charity, which is the bond of perfectness.

John 3:16- For God so loved the world, that he gave his only begotten Son, that whosoever believeth in him should not perish, but have everlasting life.

Ephesians 3:16-17- ¹⁶That he would grant you, according to the riches of his glory, to be strengthened with might by his spirit in the inner man ¹⁷That Christ may dwell in your hearts by faith; that ye, being rooted and ground in love.

Romans 12:9 Let love be without dissimulation. Abhor that which is evil; cleave to that which is good.

John 15:12- This is my commandment, that ye love one another, as I have loved you.

2 Thessalonians 3:5- And the Lord direct your hearts into the love of God, into the patient waiting for Christ.

1 Corinthians 2:9- But as it is written, eye hath not seen, nor ear heard, neither have entered into the heart of man, the things which God hath prepared fro them that love him.

Romans 8:38-39- [38]For I am persuaded, that neither death, no life, no angels, no principalities, no powers, nor things present, no things to come, [39]Nor height, no depth, no any other creature, shall be able to separate us from the love of God, which is in Christ Jesus our Lord.

DECLARATIONS

1. I declare I am open to the more of Gods love
2. I declare The Lord loves all of me, even the me I reject
3. I declare God's love is perfect and enough for me
4. I declare nothing shall separate me from the love of Jesus
5. I declare I shall grow in my love for God
6. I declare The Lord shall teach me how to love
7. I declare all hatred and bases of individuals, family members, business partners, co-workers, communities, races, other religions, things I have concluded with my own thinking, things I lack understanding in, and foreign nations shall be radically changed by the power of God's love
8. I declare all that I do shall be driven by the love of God
9. I declare my gifts shall only be stirred by my love for God and not the love of material things, money, people, or my own interest
10. I declare God's love will not be limited in me
11. I declare daily I will receive down pours of the love of God
12. I declare God's love shall drown all reject, pain, hatred, regret, oppression, heart ache, and self hatred
13. I declare I shall be an example and dispenser of God's love for all of those I come into contact with
14. I declare The Lord shall help me in areas I choose not to love in
15. I declare today that I yield to the more of Gods love
16. _____
17. _____
18. _____
19. _____

20. _____
21. _____
22. _____
23. _____
24. _____
25. _____
26. _____
27. _____
28. _____
29. _____
30. _____

PRAYER

Father, I thank You that You are God and God alone.
You are the creator of the universe and all that it contains.
High and exalted One and this day I acknowledge You.
Father, I pray, let Your will be done in my life.
Unto us, You gave us a name that is above every name; by which, every knee must bow, and every tongue must confess. By that name, I have received salvation and have obtained mercy in Your sight.
And by the name You have given us power over all things.
It is by that name and that authority I pray:
IN THE NAME OF JESUS, I yield to Your love.

Reflections

Day Twenty: I Yield to Your Glory

Many times, men, due to them not understanding what glory is, have misidentified the glory of God. What we have experiences to be glory is in most times the anointing. The anointing is something that rest and comes upon a man; glory is the manifested presence of The Father and His goodness. The anointing requires the one who was anointed but the glory just requires an audience. There is not a question that we want to be closer to God. Some of us don't know how, some of us are still battling with whole heartedly giving ourselves, and some of us just don't know if there is more to have or the importance of being closer. But I want you to know that there is so much more. There is no end to how much you can have of Him you just have to be open to receive the more of Him. When glory manifests in a room or to a people, it comes that men might encounter God's presence for themselves. The fullness of God is in His glory. We have seen Him through men, women, and songs of worship, but glory allots the opportunity for us to experience His presences with no added support.

The release and encounter of glory can be daily if we yield to seeing Him. Hunger is the breeding ground for glory. God cannot resist the hunger of His people. Yielding is the first step, but in order to manifest glory you have to want Him more than anything. You must yield in hunger. Let's yield today!

SCRIPTURES

Psalms 24:7-8 ⁷Life up your heads, O gates, and be lifted up, O ancient doors, That the King of Glory may come in! ⁸Who is the King of Glory? The Lord strong and mighty, the Lord mighty in battle

Psalms 104:1 Bless the Lord, O my soul! O Lord my God, you are very great; you are clothed with splendor and majesty

Psalms 19:10- The heavens declare the glory of God; and the firmament sheweth his handiwork

Habakkuk 2:14- For the earth shall be filled with the knowledge of the glory of the Lord, as the waters cover the sea.

Isaiah 42:8- I am the Lord: that is my name: and my glory will I not give to another, neither my praise to graven images.

Psalms 63:1-2 ¹O God, thou art my God; early will I seek thee: my soul thirsteth for thee, my flesh longeth for thee in a dry and thirsty land, where no water is; ²To see thy power and they glory, so as I have seen thee in the sanctuary.

Isaiah 60: 1-2- ¹Arise, shine; for thy light is come, and the glory of the Lord is risen upon thee. ²For, behold, the darkness shall cover the earth, and gross darkness, the people: but the Lord shall arise upon thee, and his glory shall be seen upon thee.

Romans 3:22-23- ²²Even the righteousness of God which is by faith of Jesus Christ unto all and upon all them that believe: for there is no difference: ²³For all have sinned, and come short of the glory of God.

DECLARATIONS

1. I declare the glory of the Lord in my life
2. I declare I shall experience the glory of the Lord daily
3. I declare glory shall be my regard
4. I declare a greater hunger for the glory of the Lord
5. I declare God's goodness in all things in my life
6. I declare God's glory shall overshadow my life
7. I declare glory in my prayers and intercession
8. I declare my life shall display the glory of the Lord
9. I declare glory shall make itself known in difficult times
10. I declare glory shall bring my enemies to shame
11. I declare glory shall reveal more of God to me
12. I declare glory shall manifest in my worship
13. I declare strength to stand in glory
14. I declare the revealing of God's glory in me
15. I declare today that I yield to the glory of the Lord in my life
16. _____
17. _____
18. _____
19. _____
20. _____
21. _____
22. _____
23. _____
24. _____
25. _____
26. _____
27. _____
28. _____
29. _____
30. _____

Prayer

Father, I thank You that You are God and God alone.
You are the creator of the universe and all that it contains.
High and exalted One and this day I acknowledge You.
Father, I pray, let Your will be done in my life.
Unto us, You gave us a name that is above every name; by which, every knee must bow, and every tongue must confess. By that name, I have received salvation and have obtained mercy in Your sight.
And by the name You have given us power over all things.
It is by that name and that authority I pray:
IN THE NAME OF JESUS, I yield to Your glory.

REFLECTIONS

Day Twenty-One: I Yield to Your Covenant (The Blood)

Salvation comes with many benefits that's given to the believers daily, but what makes these benefits available- even salvation itself is the shedding of blood that was fulfilled at Calvary's cross. Jesus is known as the ultimate sacrifice given that all might be redeemed unto the Father. That day and in that moment covenant was made with God and the world! Not just you and I but the universe and all that it contains. Romans 8:22 declares something powerful: "For the creature was made subject to vanity, not willingly, but by reason of Him who hath subjected the same in hope."

This redemption was not just for man but everything that was given unto man. When man transgressed against God, man was not the only one who was made subject to vanity but all of creations. However, when God redeemed man, He also redeemed all that was subjected to man. This act of unrestrained love is still prevailing for humanity whether acknowledged or not. Yielding to Christ's covenant doesn't just save you it gives you the power to overcome the wicked one, it protects you, covers you, aids you, shields you, and enables you. Moving in ignorance of Christ blood opens you to violations and assaults that cripple your progress and over all view of God's plan for your life. Let the veil be lifted and see that this covenant has not been broken but its forever. The blood shall ever remain in power over you and Gods creation. Let's yield together.

SCRIPTURES

Deuteronomy 31:8- And the Lord, he it is that doth go before thee; he will be with thee, he will not fail thee, neither forsake thee: fear not, neither be dismayed

Deuteronomy 7:9- Know therefore that the Lord thy God, he is God, the faithful God, which keepeth covenant and mercy with them that love him and keep his commandments to a thousand generations.

Psalm 103:17-18- [17]But the mercy of the Lord is from everlasting to everlasting upon them that fear him, and his righteousness unto children's children; [18]To such as keep his covenant and to those that remember his commandments to do them.

Exodus 19:5- Now therefore, if ye will obey my voice indeed, and keep my covenant, then ye shall be a peculiar treasure unto me above all people: for all the earth is mine.

Hebrews 13:20-21- [20]Now the God of peace, that brought again from the dead our Lord Jesus, through the blood of the everlasting covenant, [21]Make you perfect in every good work to do his will, working in you that which is well pleasing in his sight, through Jesus Chris; to whom be gory for ever and every. Amen.

Psalms 106:45- And he remembered for them his covenant, and repented according to the multitude of his mercies.

Psalms 89:34- My covenant will I not break, nor alter the thing that is gone out of my lips.

Isaiah 54:10- For the mountains shall depart, and the hills be removed; but my kindness shall not depart from thee, neither shall the covenant of my peace be removed, saith the Lord that hath mercy on thee.

DECLARATIONS

1. I declare Gods covenant in my life
2. I declare the blood shall protect me from all things that seeks to harm me
3. I declare the blood of Jesus shall be upon my immediate family and extended family
4. I declare the blood of Jesus shall cause me to prevail over the wicked
5. I declare my soul has been washed in the blood of Jesus
6. I declare the blood of Jesus shall cleanse me from all unrighteousness
7. I declare the blood of Jesus over my body from things that will seek to ill it
8. I declare the blood of Jesus has redeemed me from all works of evil and unrighteousness
9. I declare my life shall never be without the blood of Jesus
10. I declare the blood of Jesus shall redeem those that I love that are lost in sin
11. I declare Jesus is the lamb that was slain for my sin and His blood has redeemed me
12. I declare my life is submitted to Christ covenant in his blood
13. I declare the blood of Jesus shall be against any spirit that seeks to feast on my soul
14. I declare the blood of Jesus shall shield my mind, guard my heart, and cover my path
15. I declare today that I yield to God's covenant in my life
16. _____
17. _____
18. _____
19. _____

20. _____
21. _____
22. _____
23. _____
24. _____
25. _____
26. _____
27. _____
28. _____
29. _____
30. _____

Prayer

Father, I thank You that You are God and God alone.
You are the creator of the universe and all that it contains.
High and exalted One and this day I acknowledge You.
Father, I pray, let Your will be done in my life.
Unto us, You gave us a name that is above every name; by which, every knee must bow, and every tongue must confess. By that name, I have received salvation and have obtained mercy in Your sight.
And by the name You have given us power over all things.
It is by that name and that authority I pray:
IN THE NAME OF JESUS, I yield to Your covenant.

REFLECTIONS

Day Twenty-Two: I Yield to Your Humility

Resist, a word that houses rejection, separations, distance, no longer close, breakage and the like. In the beginning of this inspired writing, we discovered that when a person surrenders it is the discontinuation of resisting the thing or power that is greater than you. We also enlisted that this power of resistance should not be broken whether altered into another place as we yield, and that was against the enemy. However, there is something that one must acknowledged and understand there is one whom God resists too. Pride is considered one of the characteristics in man that can cause a separation between the Creator and the creation.

> 1 Peter 5:5 "Likewise, ye younger, submit yourselves unto the elder. Yea, all of you be subject one to another, and be clothed with humility: for God resisteth the proud, and giveth grace to the humble."

Yes, it is a sure thing that God will reject you, block you, and hinder you, from Him when you are prideful. Some would say I'm sweet or I am a nice person, but pride has it subtleties and breeding spaces. Pride comes to the people that feel the need to assert himself or herself over a person of authority, or when God has given instructions and you have manipulated them to make yourself comfortable. These just a few "blind spots" give entry into our lives as pride manifest. Pride will make you esteem yourself higher than you ought, walk in roles and a know it all mentality, unable to take correction, provokes you to rebellion, and most of all keeps telling you to show everyone you are okay while inside you are screaming for help.

Pride will provoke you to be a perfectionist in efforts

to keep this image of yourself before others. God rejects the proud! Some might say, "I'm not prideful." And my question to you is- if God speaks to you to bow in worship while everyone else is standing will you do it? Or if he tells you to confess your faults to your brother or sister could you do it? If God told you to submit to someone else's wisdom besides those that you feel are "worthy" to listen too, would you? If God told you not to define yourself in the mist of accusation and confusion, would you obey Him? These are just a few but I challenge you to be honest with yourself and ask God to show you were pride might be in your heart and to up root it. Let's yield together!

SCRIPTURES

Ephesians 4:2-With all lowliness and meekness, with longsuffering, forbearing one another in love

James 4:10- Humble yourselves in the sight of the Lord, and he shall lift you up.

Colossians 3:12- Put on therefore, as the elect of God, holy and beloved, bowels of mercies, kindness, humbleness of mind, meekness, longsuffering.

Proverbs 22:4- By humility and the fear of the Lord are riches, honor, and life.

1 Peter 5:6- Humble yourselves therefore under the mighty hand of god, that he may exalt you in due time.

2 Chronicles 7:14- If my people, which are called by my name, shall humble themselves, and pray, and seek my face, and turn from their wicked ways; then will I hear from heaven, and will forgive their sin, and will heal their land.

Proverbs 15:33- The fear of the Lord is the instruction of wisdom; and before honor is humility.

John 3:30- He must increase, but I must decrease

Psalms 149:4- For the Lord taketh pleasure in his people: he will beautify the meek with salvation.

DECLARATIONS

1. I declare I have the humility of God
2. I declare all pride known and unknown shall be revealed to me
3. I declare new grace in my obedience to the voice of God
4. I declare I will be humble even in my upraising
5. I declare pride has broken off of my life in all areas as it is revealed
6. I declare I shall be more discipline in my humility
7. I declare The Lord shall make me aware of areas I am proud in
8. I declare pride shall no longer hinder me from places of service
9. I declare my heart shall be at ease when I am challenged in things that offend my pride
10. I declare I will not be opposed to learning things from those that I may feel are not "on my level" of knowledge, education, thinking, and maturity
11. I declare all pride that was taught to me by those in authority over me is now broken in Jesus name
12. I declare I will be a servant even as Jesus was
13. I declare I will decrease that Christ might increase in me
14. I declare pride shall not lead me to great falls! For the covenant with pride and my life has been broken.
15. I declare I have yielded to the humility of God
16. _____
17. _____
18. _____
19. _____
20. _____
21. _____
22. _____

23. _____
24. _____
25. _____
26. _____
27. _____
28. _____
29. _____
30. _____

Prayer

Father, I thank You that You are God and God alone.
You are the creator of the universe and all that it contains.
High and exalted One and this day I acknowledge You.
Father, I pray, let Your will be done in my life.
Unto us, You gave us a name that is above every name; by which, every knee must bow, and every tongue must confess. By that name, I have received salvation and have obtained mercy in Your sight.
And by the name You have given us power over all things.
It is by that name and that authority I pray:
IN THE NAME OF JESUS, I yield to Your humility.

REFLECTIONS

Day Twenty-Three: I Yield to Your Patience

I'm sure most of us have been faced with a co-worker, children's schoolteacher, boss, or even extended family whose personalities are uniquely different from your own. This can be in their interactions or even in their way of doing things that differs from yours. Either way this challenges you to remain genuine when engaging with these kinds of people. Now there are two kinds of people that will be reading this: those that have a hard time being patient with those that think differently, respond differently or in manners that seem to be a "waste" of time, or those that are very patient with others but have very little patients with themselves.

Those that have little patience with themselves are dealing with the same characteristics as the first described, the difference is it is just directed towards you. There is no self-forgiveness when it comes to the areas you are seeking to grow in and or change. We must yield to God kind of patience. This trait of endurance, long-suffering, and mercy is something God shows us all of our days. Let's be an extension of that to others and ourselves. Let's yield together!

SCRIPTURES

Proverbs 14:29- He that is slow to wrath is of great understanding: but he hat is hasty of spirit exalteth folly.

Romans 12:12- Rejoicing in hope; patient in tribulation; continuing instant in prayer

Galatians 6:9- And let us not be weary in well doing: for in due season we shall reap, if we faint not.

Psalms 37-7- Rest in the Lord, and wait patiently for him: fret not thyself because of him who prospereth in his way, because of the man who bringeth wicked devices to pass.

Psalms 27:14- Wait on the Lord: be of good courage, and he shall strengthen thine heart: wait, I say, on the Lord.

Exodus 14:14- The Lord shall fight for you, and ye shall hold your peace.

2 Peter 3:9- The Lord is not slack concerning his promise, as some men count slackness; but is longsuffering to us-ward, not willing that nay should perish, but that all should come to repentance.

Joel 2:13- And rend your heart, and not your garments, and turn unto the Lord you God: for his gracious and merciful, slow to anger, and of great kindness, and repenteth him of the evil.

2 Peter 3:8- But, beloved, be not ignorant of this one things, that one day is with the Lord as a thousand years, and a thousand years as one day.

DECLARATIONS

1. I declare I have God kind of patience
2. I declare I will not be quick to be angry
3. I declare I have an understanding heart
4. I declare patience shall protect me from making hasty decisions
5. I declare I will honor others process of growth by being patient with them
6. I declare patience shall be given unto me by those that look to me
7. I declare patience will not be a attribute I chose to walk in when it most convenient
8. I declare I will be patient even when its not shown to me
9. I declare I shall be patient in affliction
10. I declare in times of trouble I will wait patiently for the Lord
11. I declare I will be still while the Lord fights for me
12. I declare patience shall find me when I am being stretch
13. I declare may I endure hardness with patience
14. I declare patience is my weapon of choice when faced with things that seem to tarry, knowing that my end has already been secured
15. I declare today that I yield to God's kind of patience
16. _____
17. _____
18. _____
19. _____
20. _____
21. _____
22. _____
23. _____
24. _____

25. _____
26. _____
27. _____
28. _____
29. _____
30. _____

Prayer

Father, I thank You that You are God and God alone.
You are the creator of the universe and all that it contains.
High and exalted One and this day I acknowledge You.
Father, I pray, let Your will be done in my life.
Unto us, You gave us a name that is above every name; by which, every knee must bow, and every tongue must confess. By that name, I have received salvation and have obtained mercy in Your sight.
And by the name You have given us power over all things.
It is by that name and that authority I pray:
IN THE NAME OF JESUS, I yield to Your patience.

REFLECTIONS

Day Twenty-Four: I Yield to Your **Revenge**

We live in a world of free will. One of the greatest things that God has given to man is choice, yet it is the most dangerous. This thing that we call will can either be an expression of us freely giving to God or an open sign of our rebellion. With that being said, I have had many none believers state to me that if there was a God why does He allow bad things to happen? And my response has always been, its not God that allows bad things happen, it's people that do bad things. Most of us have had things to be done to us, our families, communities, and nation but those that are evil, however, is it our job to seek vengeances?

God makes it very clear in his word that it's not our job to render evil for evil but it is our job to remain vessels of honor and instruments of peace. Now I know a lot of us don't pursue the vengeance that was in our hearts, however, it was thought, said, wished, and even sometimes prayed. Let's yield this place to the Lord that He might save our hearts from thoughts of hatred and wishing the downfall of those are we called to love even when they have wronged us. Let's yield together!

SCRIPTURES

Romans 12-19- Dearly beloved, avenge not yourselves, but [rather] give place unto wrath: for it is written, vengeance [is] mine; I will repay.

1 Peter 3:9- Not rendering evil for evil, or railing for railing: but contrariwise blessing; knowing that ye are thereunto called, that ye should inherit a blessing.

Proverbs 24:29- Say not, I will do so to him as he hath done to me: I will render to the man according to his work.

Leviticus 19:18- Thou shalt not avenge, nor bear any grudge against the children of thy people, but thou shalt love thy neighbor as thyself: I [am] the LORD.

Mark 11:25- And when ye stand praying, forgive, if ye have ought against any: that your Father also which is in heaven may forgive you your trespasses

1 Peter 2:23- Who, wen he was reviled, reviled not again; when he suffered, he threatened not; but committed [himself] to him that judgeth righteously.

Romans 13:4- For he is the minister of God to thee for good. But if thou do that which is evil be afraid; for he beareth not the sword in vain: for he is the minister of God, a revenger to [execute] wrath upon him that doeth evil.

1 Thessalonians 5:15- See that none render evil for evil unto any [man]; but ever follow that which is good, both among yourselves, and to all [men].

DECLARATIONS

1. I declare I yield all spirits of revenge in my Father
2. I declare I will not be quick to anger
3. I declare revenge is kept in the hands of an all knowing God
4. I declare all thoughts that wishes others down fall has been removed from my heart
5. I declare God judges all things including the wicked
6. I declare I have a love that reaches the places of me that hurt and want revenge
7. I declare may my heart be full of compassion to those that assault me
8. I declare I will strive to do good to others
9. I declare the Lord shall have His revenge on the wicked therefore I will not seek out my own
10. I declare all hidden places in my heart that do not want me to forgive someone, may that place of their offence is be burned by the spirit of God
11. I declare the wicked shall have their day of judgment
12. I declare evil works done against me and those I love shall not go without the Lord's eye seeing and knowing
13. I declare all retaliation against those who have wrong me has be removed from my heart now
14. I declare any part of my soul that would seek to with hold resource for those that have wronged me in order to punish them for their actions has been broken
15. I declare my heavenly Father fights for me
16. _____
17. _____
18. _____
19. _____
20. _____

21. _____
22. _____
23. _____
24. _____
25. _____
26. _____
27. _____
28. _____
29. _____
30. _____

Prayer

Father, I thank You that You are God and God alone.
You are the creator of the universe and all that it contains.
High and exalted One and this day I acknowledge You.
Father, I pray, let Your will be done in my life.
Unto us, You gave us a name that is above every name; by which, every knee must bow, and every tongue must confess. By that name, I have received salvation and have obtained mercy in Your sight.
And by the name You have given us power over all things.
It is by that name and that authority I pray:
IN THE NAME OF JESUS, I yield to Your revenge.

Reflections

Day Twenty-Five: I Yield to Your Usage

Our day-to-day lives are filled with tasks that have been ordained by roles. These roles are expected of us whether we want to fulfill them or not. Being a mother, father, sibling, co-worker, leader, and neighbor are just a few roles that we render. However, these roles can have such a great demand that we opt out of the services and use to God to maintain our lives. The service of God doesn't come to remove you from these roles however it will challenge you in them.

Yielding your life to the use of the Father may at times seem inconvenience, untimely, hard, difficult and even counter productive. The word of God assures us that the greatest in the Kingdom is a servant. Even Jesus Himself didn't come into the world to be served but He came to serve. We see throughout the life of Jesus His reckless abandonment for the common things of the world and His dedication to the cause of His father. As you yield yourself to the use of the Father, you set your heart to join a cause greater than yourself and to glorify a King. Let's yield together!

SCRIPTURES

Ephesians 5:15-16- [15]See then that ye walk circumspectly, not as fools, but as wise, [16]Redeeming the time because the days are evil

Colossians 3:23-24- [23]And whatsoever ye do, do it heartily, as to the Lord, and not unto men; [24]Knowing that of the Lord ye shall receive the reward of the inheritance: for ye serve the Lord Christ

Mark 8:36- For what shall it profit a man, if he shall gain the whole world, and lose his own soul?

Psalm 31:3- For thou art my rock and my fortress; therefore for thy name's sake lead me and guide me

Romans 12:2- And be not conformed to this world: but be ye transformed by the renewing of your mind, that ye may prove what is that good, and acceptable and perfect, will of God.

Proverbs 4:23- Keep thy heart with all diligence; for out of it are the issues of life

Proverbs 13:3- He that keepeth his mouth keepeth his life: but he that openeth wide his lips shall have destruction.

Galatians 2:20- I am crucified with Christ: nevertheless I live; yet not I, but Christ liveth in me: and the life which I now live in the flesh I live by the faith of the Son of God, who loved me, and gave himself for me.

Proverbs 19:8- He that getteth wisdom loveth his own soul: he that keepeth understanding shall find good.

DECLARATIONS

1. I declare I yield myself to the usage of God
2. I declare I will be used of The Lord in all things that I do
3. I declare I will have a great sensitivity to the Lord's voice
4. I declare, this day I yield my life roles to the use of the Lord
5. I declare the Lord shall get the glory out of my life
6. I declare I will not be driven by my emotions but obedient to God's use
7. I declare my want is to do the will of Him that sent me, Christ Jesus
8. I declare I will reply on God's spirit and not my own in all things
9. I declare a greater desire shall come upon me daily to be used of the Lord
10. I declare fear of failing has been removed from my heart
11. I declare the courage to pursue the cause the Lord will lead me too
12. I declare every part of my being is available to be used by God
13. I declare I am the servant of the Lord
14. I declare my heart will carry the burdens of the Lord for His people and His Church
15. I declare I shall be used of God to glorify His Kingdom
16. _____
17. _____
18. _____
19. _____
20. _____
21. _____

22. _____
23. _____
24. _____
25. _____
26. _____
27. _____
28. _____
29. _____
30. _____

Prayer

Father, I thank You that You are God and God alone.
You are the creator of the universe and all that it contains.
High and exalted One and this day I acknowledge You.
Father, I pray, let Your will be done in my life.
Unto us, You gave us a name that is above every name; by which, every knee must bow, and every tongue must confess. By that name, I have received salvation and have obtained mercy in Your sight.
And by the name You have given us power over all things.
It is by that name and that authority I pray:
IN THE NAME OF JESUS, I yield to Your use.

REFLECTIONS

Day Twenty-Six: I Yield to Your **Deliverance**

Deliverance for many has been looked at as a bad thing and not a closer thing. Deliverance has gained a reputation of something being wrong with the person that is being delivered. However, deliverance is a ministry that has been given to us to bring us closer to the Father. Spiritual powers that are enemies of our souls seek to keep us entangled in the traps, alternate identities, fears, oppression, rejection, heath problems all in the name to keep us from manifesting Christ in us and around us. Christ finished work on the cross has already condemned and judged these powers, but they still seek to corrupt us to join their judgments; pulling us further away from our newness of life.

Yielding to deliverance helps to bring you to a place called close. This doesn't mean that God is far from you when you are in places of challenge or fault. It does mean that the more deliverance you have, the more of you He has. Entering into that freedom and not settle for the things of your past. God longs to deliver us out of every oppressive trap of the enemy, we just have to yield to it. Let's yield together!

SCRIPTURES

Psalms 34:17- [The righteous] cry, and the LORD heareth, and delivereth them out of all their troubles.

Galatians 5:1- Stand fast therefore in the liberty wherewith Christ has made us free, and be not entangled again with the yoke of bondage.

2 Peter 2:9- The Lord knoweth how to deliver the godly out of temptations, and to reserve the unjust unto the day of judgment to be punished

Matthew 10:1- And when he had called unto [him] his twelve disciples, he gave them power [against] unclean spirits, to cast them out, and to heal all manner of sickness and all manner of disease.

Psalms 107:6- Then they cried unto the LORD in their trouble, [and] he delivered them out of their distresses.

2 Samuel 22:2- and he said, The LORD [is] my rock, and my fortress, and my deliverer

Psalms 18:7- He delivered me from my strong enemy, and from them which hated me: for they were too strong for me

Psalms 40:2- He brought me up also out of an horrible pit, out of the miry clay, and set my feet upon a rock, and established my goings.

Colossians 1:13- Who hath delivered us from the power of darkness, and hath translated us into the kingdom of his dear son

Psalms 51:17- The sacrifices of God are a broken spirit: a broken and a contrite heart, O God, thou wilt not despise

DECLARATIONS

1. I declare my soul is a direct recipient of God's deliverance
2. I declare I shall have God deliverance in every area of my life
3. I declare the Lord shall reveal areas of challenges to me that I need freedom in
4. I declare I will not oppose the deliverance power of God
5. I declare all fear of confession and accepting the truth of soul issues have been broken by Christ power
6. I declare I shall walk daily in the delivering power of God
7. I declare my soul is free from wombs of the past in all things
8. I declare my soul rejoices at the chastening of The Lord
9. I declare deliverance shall bring me closer to my Father that I might see Him inside of me
10. I declare all evil works of the carnal man shall be far from me for I have the spirit of God living in me
11. I declare my time of freedom is now
12. I declare deliverance is my filter of purifying my soul
13. I declare all fear of deliverance is broken from my mind and spirit
14. I declare I will have no allegiance to any power, person, social group, or self cause that will seek to hinder my pursuit of Christ deliverance
15. I declare I yield my soul to God's deliverance
16. _____
17. _____
18. _____
19. _____
20. _____

21. _____
22. _____
23. _____
24. _____
25. _____
26. _____
27. _____
28. _____
29. _____
30. _____

Prayer

Father, I thank You that You are God and God alone.
You are the creator of the universe and all that it contains.
High and exalted One and this day I acknowledge You.
Father, I pray, let Your will be done in my life.
Unto us, you gave us a name that is above every name; by which, every knee must bow, and every tongue must confess. By that name, I have received salvation and have obtained mercy in Your sight.
And by the name You have given us power over all things.
It is by that name and that authority I pray:
IN THE NAME OF JESUS, I yield to Your deliverance.

REFLECTIONS

Day Twenty-Seven: I Yield to Your Infilling

Jesus died on the cross to redeem us from our sins, but that was not all that took place after His finished work. All separation between God and man was now removed and we are now afforded the opportunity to go before God's throne ourselves. But it still doesn't stop there. Now we don't just have the opportunity to God to the Father but we can be filled with Him. This eternal, all power, all knowing, everlasting God has chosen to make us His temple and dwelling place.

Christ habitation in us allows us to be a walking encounter. This infilling gives us more of Him to pour out on all that we come into contact with. Yielding in being filled with the more of God takes you to the depths of His spirit. As you yield today set your heart to becoming one burning for the more of Him, asking though your cup is filled still wanting more of Him. Let's yield together!

SCRIPTURES

Acts 4:31- And when they had prayed, the place was shaken where they were assembled together; and they were all filled with the Holy Ghost, and they spake the word of God with boldness

Ephesians 5:18- And be not drunk with wine, wherein is excess; but be filled with the Spirit.

Romans 5:5- And hope maketh not ashamed; because the love of God is shed abroad in our hearts by the Holy Ghost which is given unto us.

John 14:26- But the Comforter, [which is] the Holy Ghost, whom the Father will send in my name, he shall teach you all things, and bring all things to your remembrance, whatsoever I have said unto you.

Acts 1:8- But ye shall receive power, after that the Holy Ghost is come upon you: and ye shall be witnesses unto me both in Jerusalem, and in all Judaea, and in Samaria, and unto the uttermost part of the earth.

1 Corinthians 6:19- What? Know ye not that your body is the temple of the Holy Ghost [which is] in you, which ye have of God, and ye are not your own?

Acts 2:4- And they were all filled with the Holy Ghost, and began to speak with other tongues, as the Spirit gave them utterance.

Exodus 31:3- And I have filled him with the spirit of God in wisdom, and in understanding, and in knowledge, and in all manner of workmanship

Ezekiel 36: 27- And I will put my spirit within you, and cause you to walk in my statutes, and ye shall keep my judgments, and do them.

2 Timothy 1:14- That good thing which was committed unto thee, keep by the Holy Ghost which dwelleth in us.

DECLARATIONS

1. I declare my soul and spirit shall yield to the infilling of God's spirit
2. I declare I have a renewed hunger for the Lord daily
3. I declare I am not afraid of God filling
4. I declare all forms of complacency and contentment have been broken by God's power
5. I declare I shall be full and want no more
6. I declare no desire shall be greater than my desire for God
7. I declare a great passion is open to me this day
8. I declare my soul longs for the living God
9. I declare the Lord is enough for me
10. I declare I shall be an example of a spirit filled life
11. I declare my loved ones shall be filled with God's spirit
12. I declare God's spirit lives in the members of my soul
13. I declare all powers that seek to rob me of my filling have been destroyed in Jesus name
14. I declare I am filled with all that God is
15. I declare I yield my soul and spirit to the infilling of Gods spirit
16. _____
17. _____
18. _____
19. _____
20. _____
21. _____
22. _____
23. _____
24. _____
25. _____
26. _____
27. _____

28. _____
29. _____
30. _____

Prayer

Father, I thank You that You are God and God alone.
You are the creator of the universe and all that it contains.
High and exalted One and this day I acknowledge You.
Father, I pray, let Your will be done in my life.
Unto us, You gave us a name that is above every name; by which, every knee must bow, and every tongue must confess. By that name, I have received salvation and have obtained mercy in Your sight.
And by the name You have given us power over all things.
It is by that name and that authority I pray:
IN THE NAME OF JESUS I yield to Your infilling.

REFLECTIONS

Day Twenty-Eight: I Yield to Your **Baptism**

Baptism has been viewed from a one-dimensional perspective not knowing that there is a baptism that we can have everyday. The focus of any baptism is to be completely submerged and to come up from that submerging new. There are spiritual baptisms that we can take daily where our lives are completely submerged in the spirit of God. There also are baptisms that come to submerge us in anger, frustration, pain, anxiety, depression, and oppression in efforts to get our lives to be completely submerged in an issue that is counter productive to our destinies.

As you yield today I say open yourself willingly to God's baptism that you might be fully submerge in Him. It's like taking a bath in the pool of God. You are not just feeling Him or experiencing Him in certain parts of you, you feel and sense Him in everything! Your hearing, smell, touch, taste, mind, soul, and heart! Everything has been wrecked by this overwhelming baptism.

SCRIPTURES

Galatians 3:26-27- [26]For ye are all the children of God by faith in Christ Jesus. [27]For as many of you as have been baptized into Christ have put on Christ.

Matthew 28:19-20- [19]Go ye therefore, and teach all nations, baptizing them in the name of the Father, and of the Son, and of the Holy Ghost; [20]Teaching them to observe all things whatsoever I have commanded you: and, lo, I am with you always, even unto the end of the world. Amen

1 Corinthians 12:13- For by one Spirit are we all baptized into one body, whether we be Jews or Gentiles, whether we be bond or free: and have been all made to drink into one Spirit

1 Peter 3:21- The like figure whereunto even baptism doth also now save us (not the putting away of the filth of the flesh, but the answer of a good conscience toward God,) by the resurrection of Jesus Christ.

John 3:5- Jesus answered, Verily, verily, I say unto thee, Except a man be born of water and of the Spirit, he cannon enter into the kingdom of God

Acts 22:16- And now why tarriest thou? Arise, and be baptized, and wash away thy sins, calling on the name of the Lord

John 1:33- And I know him not: but he that sent me to baptize with water, the same said unto me, Upon whom thou shalt see the Spirit descending, and remaining on him, the same is he which baptizeth with the Holy Ghost.

Mark 16:16- he that believeth and is baptized shall be save; but he that believeth not shall be damned

DECLARATIONS

1. I declare I shall be baptized everyday in God's spirit
2. I declare God's baptism shall provoke the release of God's nature in me
3. I declare I shall be baptized that I might be in Him
4. I declare I will not be submerged in frustration, anger, pain, worry, anxiety, fear, emotional hardship, distress, misunderstanding, and folly. For there is only one baptism that my life shall partake of; the baptism of God's spirit
5. I declare I have been baptized therefore I shall be saved in my day of trouble, adversity, strive, contention, resistance, and retaliation
6. I declare baptism is always an option when wanting to receive more of God
7. I declare I will not resist God's baptism
8. I declare I shall have a fresh baptism of fire
9. I declare by baptism shall I be submerged in glory
10. I declare I shall experience baptisms everyday in worship, prayer, intercession, and love
11. I declare baptism has caused me to put on Christ
12. I declare I have been baptized into one Spirit, Christ's spirit
13. I declare nothing by any means shall keep me away from baptism
14. I declare all fear of complete submerging in God has been removed and replace with boldness that is given to me daily
15. I declare I shall yield to the daily baptism of God's spirit
16. _____
17. _____
18. _____
19. _____

20. _____
21. _____
22. _____
23. _____
24. _____
25. _____
26. _____
27. _____
28. _____
29. _____
30. _____

Prayer

Father, I thank You that You are God and God alone.
You are the creator of the universe and all that it contains.
High and exalted One and this day I acknowledge You.
Father, I pray, let Your will be done in my life.
Unto us, You gave us a name that is above every name; by which, every knee must bow, and every tongue must confess. By that name, I have received salvation and have obtained mercy in Your sight.
And by the name You have given us power over all thing.
It is by that name and that authority I pray:
IN THE NAME OF JESUS, I yield to Your baptism.

REFLECTIONS

Day Twenty-Nine: I Yield to Your **Burden**

Prayer is one of the most foundational principles of the Lord's church. Without this essential foundational tool, we will find ourselves disconnected from things eternal. Pressures will come to burden you in your natural life in order to bring a level of distress to you in efforts to cause you to gain weary in your well doing. However, this is when prayer is most needed. Yes, praying for the things that we need is necessary, but we still have been commanded to prayer for one another. Nehemiah begins this interesting quested once this burden came for his people in prayer. The Bible begins to describe what begins to take place within Nehemiah after he hears these words about his nation. He sits down, weeps, and mourns a number of days, fasts, and prayer. And out of that place, heaven begins to charge him with a burden to rebuild.

Now, throughout scripture you will find this very thing happening to voices of influence. These burdens or loads that heaven releases, come to weigh upon us not in a bad way, but to show us the density of the charge He is giving to us in that place of prayer. Matthew 11:29 declares, " Take My yoke upon you, and learn of Me." This kind of exchange must happen in our lives that we may gain heavens agenda for our present time. Remove and release yourself from the yokes of life that you might obtain the burdens of heaven. Yielding to God's burdens eliminates the natural ones that you have for your own life and helps you to focus on things eternal. Let's yield today!

SCRIPTURES

Psalms 68:19 Blessed be the Lord, who daily loadeth us with benefits, even the God of our salvation. Selah.

Matthew 11:29-30 ^{29}Take my yoke upon you, and learn of me; for I am meek and lowly in heart: and ye shall find rest unto your souls. ^{30}For my yoke is easy, and my burden is light.

Zephaniah 3:17 The Lord thy God in the midst of thee is mighty; he will save, he will rejoice over thee with joy; he will rest in his love, he will joy over thee with singing.

Psalms 55:22 Cast thy burden upon the Lord, and he shall sustain thee: he shall never suffer the righteous to be moved.

Psalms 18:6 In my distress I called upon the Lord, and cried unto my God: he heard my voice out of his temple, and my cry came before him, even into his ears.

Psalms 50:15 And call upon me in the day of trouble: I will deliver thee, and thou shalt glorify me.

Philippians 4:6-7 ^{6}Be careful for nothing; but in every thing by prayer and supplication with thanksgiving let your requests be made known unto God. ^{7}And the peace of God, which passeth all understanding, shall keep your hearts and minds through Christ Jesus.

DECLARATIONS

1. I declare I have the burden(s) of the Lord
2. I declare I have exchanged my burdens with the Lord
3. I declare all false burdens shall be removed from me now in the name of the Lord, Jesus
4. I declare I will not hold onto the things I cannot control. I will release them to the hand of the Lord and he will help me
5. I declare may my heart be open to receive the burden of the Lord even if it challenges me
6. I declare may my heart reach the place of Heavens burden
7. I declare a renewed sensitivity to my community and those that I am called to serve
8. I declare the endurance to carry out the charge the Lord gives me by way of burden
9. I declare my life is shielded from carrying things that are meant to distract me from the purposes of God
10. I declare the Lord shall speak to my spirit and provide me with the necessary tools to accomplish all charges brought by burdens
11. I declare may my life synchronized with heaven
12. I declare I have heavens agreement in all things that I do
13. I declare the Lord has spoken unto me and I have heard it
14. I declare all voices that will come to persuade me from the will of God have been cut off from my life
15. I declare that I yield to the burden(s) of the Lord
16. _____
17. _____
18. _____
19. _____
20. _____

21. _____
22. _____
23. _____
24. _____
25. _____
26. _____
27. _____
28. _____
29. _____
30. _____

PRAYER

Father, I thank You that You are God and God alone.
You are the creator of the universe and all that it contains.
High and exalted One and this day I acknowledge You.
Father, I pray, let Your will be done in my life.
Unto us, You gave us a name that is above every name; by which, every knee must bow, and every tongue must confess.
By that name, I have received salvation and have obtained mercy in Your sight.
And by the name You have given us power over all things.
It is by that name and that authority I pray:
IN THE NAME OF JESUS, I yield to Your burden.

REFLECTIONS

Day Thirty: I Yield to Your Praise

Our lives as believers will constantly encounter this undying love that the Savior has for us as His people. It's hard to comprehend, yet so simple, strong enough to save us and die for us, yet sensitive enough to touch us when we most need it. This kind of love is hard to comprehend. But is it really for us to comprehend or just receive? The "how of His love is not as important as to the "why" of His love, and even that answer is simple; because He choose to love us. He chose us to be His and His alone. He picked us to walk in the dominion of His name, and He repents not of His choice.

We are the object of His affection, the prizes and possession of heaven, the one thing He wants, the people of His praise. Yielding in praise is more than just giving God glory because He is God and it is due His name. Yielding in praise is the response of a person, a people, a community, and a nation choosing Him back. As you open yourself to be a constant instrument of praise, you will find that this is what we were created for to choose Him back. So as we yield this final day, lets make it our primary focus in all things to give God praise. Let's yield together!

SCRIPTURES

Isaiah 25:1- O Lord, thou art my God; I will exalt thee, I will praise thy name; for thou hast done wonderful things; thy counsels of old are faithfulness and truth

Psalms 150:6- Let every thing that hath breath Praise ye the Lord.

John 4:24- God is a Spirit: and they that worship him must worship him in spirit and in truth

1 Chronicles 16:34- O give thanks unto the Lord; for he is good; for his mercy endureth forever.

Psalms 71:8- Let my mouth be filled with thy praise and with thy honour all the day.

2 Samuel 7:22- Wherefore thou art great, O Lord God: for there is none like thee, neither is there any God beside thee, according to all that we have heard with our ears

Revelation 5:13- And every creature which is in heaven, and on the earth, and under the earth, and such as are in the sea, and all that are in them, heard I saying, Blessings, and honour, and glory, and power, be unto him that sitteth upon the throne, and unto the Lamb for ever and ever.

Psalms 108:3- I will praise thee, O Lord, among the people: and I will sing praises unto thee among the nations.

Psalms 145:3- Great is the Lord, and greatly to be praised; and his greatness is unsearchable

DECLARATIONS

1. I declare I am a instrument of praise
2. I declare praise is common in my life
3. I declare I will live a life of praise
4. I declare in all things I will give thanks
5. I declare my soul shall make her boast before the Lord
6. I declare praise shall war against my enemies and bring them to shame
7. I declare my praise will not be contingent upon how I feel but it shall be directed by God's spirit alone
8. I declare I will not be ashamed to praise the Lord my God
9. I declare the Lord is good and He is worthy of my praise
10. I declare I have chosen the Lord for He has chosen me
11. I declare my house shall be a house of praise
12. I declare I will praise the Lord for He has caused me to triumph over my enemies
13. I declare my life's purpose is to praise the Lord, my creator
14. I declare I shall praise the Lord in my uprising, in the noonday, and in my down sitting. I will magnify the Lord
15. I declare today I yield my praise to my Lord, my God
16. _____
17. _____
18. _____
19. _____
20. _____
21. _____
22. _____
23. _____

24. _____
25. _____
26. _____
27. _____
28. _____
29. _____
30. _____

Prayer

Father, I thank You that You are God and God alone.
You are the creator of the universe and all that it contains.
High and exalted One and this day I acknowledge You.
Father, I pray, let Your will be done in my life.
Unto us, You gave us a name that is above every name; by which, every knee must bow, and every tongue must confess. By that name, I have received salvation and have obtained mercy in Your sight.
And by the name You have given us power over all things.
It is by that name and that authority I pray:
IN THE NAME OF JESUS, I yield to Your Praise.

REFLECTIONS

Myself, I Give, Willingly

BIBLIOGRAPHY

King James Bible, Hendrickson Publication, 2006.

Made in the USA
Lexington, KY
17 February 2018